THE BEST TIME TO PLANT A TREE

Gerry Cooney

ORIGINAL WRITING

978-1-907179-77-8

A CIP catalogue for this book is available from the National Library.

Published by Original Writing Ltd., Dublin, 2010.

Printed in the UK by MPG Books Group, Bodmin and Kings Lynn.

ACKNOWLEDGEMENTS

Particular thanks to those who shared the risk and the African adventure with me when it might have been easier to say thanks but no thanks when I needed their support. To my own brothers and sister-Hugh, Evelyn, Paul and Stan I acknowledge that it couldn't have happened without you. In fact your involvement made the experience more enjoyable. Also to Kevin Kilmurray, Pat Mc Gahern, Padraig O'Connell, Ray and Jacinta O'Brien and Stephen and Breda Mc Cormack-your support was also invaluable in order to realise the dream when it looked like it was slipping away at one stage.

Special thanks also to all those who visited Ghaub during my time there. Evelyn and Ian Mac Kenzie-Smith, Marie Mac Farlan, Pat Mc Gahern, Kevin Kilmurray, Padraig and Martina O'Connell, Allen, Mellie, Rory and Colm Moran, Pat and Siobhan Mc Bennett, Rita O' Sullivan and Mary Gannon, Jimmy Stewart, Christy and Kathleen Hand, Johnny Grehan, Martin Minnock, Chris and Mary Glennon, Christy and Mary Reynolds, James and Audrey Tallon, Sean Sherlock and Joe Mc Kenna. Definitely the most enjoyable time for me was when Irish friends visited and I could share this adventure and the delights of this incredible place with them. We had some great laughs and the Irish certainly made an impression on the people of Namibia. International relations between the two countries have grown considerably and many Namibians have a greater appreciation of all things Irish as a result. I would also like to thank all the friends I made in Namibia who welcomed me into their lives and homes with such generosity. Too many to mention individually but I will never forget Alex, Roswitha, Alan, Gesa, Vera, Mike, Sonya, Billy, and Judith who helped in their own individual way to make the experience so memorable. I would also like to mention especially the Compion family who were always there for me when I needed them. I hope that my story may encourage more Irish people to visit Namibia in the future and perhaps spread the word about this beautiful welcoming country. Pictures by Alan and Gesa Hendry and Leonie Van Niekerk. Illustrations by Roswitha Tretter.

Synopsis

In August 2007 I visited Namibia in South West Africa with my wife Marian and our three boys Anthony, Christopher and Garth. We had planned a family holiday to Africa as we wanted this year to be special and unlike previous family holidays to the sun. We also had relations in Namibia which made it an easier choice .I had been there once before many years ago when I had ventured off for three weeks in 1982 to visit family and explore some of the country that until then had been a bit of a mystery to me. Namibia made quite an impression and I promised to return but didn't expect that it would take me more than 25 years. We planned an interesting itinerary with something for everyone and headed off with high hopes. During the course of our trip we stayed in a small lodge for two nights called Guest Farm Ghaub located in the North of the country roughly ninety minute from the Etosha Wildlife Park. I cannot honestly say if it was instant but definitely soon after we arrived I realised that we were in a special place and was blown away by the sheer beauty of the farm and the peaceful atmosphere that existed there. I fell in love with the place and somehow felt at home. I really believed that this magical place found us as much as we found it and when we discovered that the lodge and farm was for sale it seemed that this was an opportunity that could not be passed up. Over the following two months we struggled with the idea of making a major life change and a significant financial investment to secure the property and possibly our future. It came together through some hard work, support from family and friends and several strokes of luck. We signed for the lodge and farm on December 1st and my life was about to change drastically as I took leave of absence from my job as an Addiction counsellor at the Rutland Treatment Centre in Dublin.

I spent the best part of fifteen months alone without my family setting up the business and working in an incredible country with incredible people. This book is an account of my experiences there which were marked with unbelievable highs but also with some dark moments. I hope the story might be of interest to others for a number of reasons. Firstly it's an ordinary story about an ordinary person in an extraordinary place. It's about living in Africa which is special and Namibia particularly which is certainly one of the gems of the African continent. It's about having a gap year at fifty years of age and taking the plunge to do something very different. It's also about the demands of taking on a new challenge and carrying the responsibility of developing a business without any experience and precious little time to learn. It's also about coping away from home without the support and company of your family in a country with very different cultural beliefs. It's definitely about self exploration and introspective soul searching when it's very uncomfortable to be left alone with your own thoughts for long stretches of time.

I hope it might inspire someone to take a chance and follow their dream. The experience has been life changing for me and it's largely to do with the people I have met during my time in Namibia. I have learned so much from the staff at the lodge about humility, patience and forbearance. The guests and patrons have been both a pleasure and a challenge as the service industry brings you in contact with some fantastic appreciative people and also some others that you could never please. The children and the Sisters at the local school who I befriended have restored my belief in something spiritual which I had lost in recent years. They are the real heroes of the story and that is why I would like to donate all proceeds accrued from the sale of this publication towards the continued education and welfare of the children of Maria Bronn School in Grootfontein, Namibia.

Gerry C.

Contents

Introduction

It started on a whim but became a reality. One of those opportunities that is easier to turn down. There have been a few over the years. The house in the country about an hour from Dublin with outhouses and room for a pony! We looked at it but decided against it. I have thought more than once about how life might have been very different! The holiday home in Kerry overlooking the sea at Ballyheigue was another. Once owned by renowned Irish writer Christy Brown. Absolutely true. It was going for a song and perched on the cliff tops overlooking the beach it was such a beautiful location and could have made a magical home from home. It took me a while to let that one go and I often had regrets about not taking the plunge. Then more recently there was the mobile home near Curracloe beach in Wexford which a friend was selling. Only two hours from Dublin I imagined we could be there before 7.00pm on a Friday evening for long week-ends in the sunny south East. It wasn't meant to be and it was just the wrong time for us. So there have been a few what ifs, if only, what might have been? However I always believed that someday an opportunity would come along. I was destined to live in the country at some stage of my life and keep animals. A pipedream perhaps but somehow, somewhere, sometime I believed it would happen. Then out of the blue in August 2007 it did happen and I knew immediately that this was the opportunity I was waiting for. Guest Farm Ghaub found us as much as we found it during a family holiday to Namibia in South West Africa.

It really began shortly after Christmas 2006 when we sat down as a family to discuss our holiday options for the coming year. Over dinner one Sunday evening we began to chat about it and everyone had their own ideas. In previous years we had gone boating on the Shannon which we loved. We had been to Spain a couple of times and I suppose our trip to Florida in 2004 had been the highlight to date which the boys particularly enjoyed.

Maybe this year we would try somewhere different as the lads were getting older and this could be our last real family holiday as such. What about Africa I suggested not knowing how the family would react. The boys have always been interested in animals and wildlife and the prospect of going on Safari would surely appeal to them. Marian would enjoy the guaranteed good weather and I was thinking of the desert and the long drives on empty roads. Having cousins in Namibia made it possible and it seemed like a great opportunity to experience the magic of Africa and visit our Namibian relations at the same time. It was pretty much agreed there and then and we began to make our plans for a three week trip in July or August. It would have to be three weeks this year as it is such a long way to travel for less. Also we imagined there would be so much to see that we would need that much time to sample "The Big Empty" as Namibia is sometimes called. I have since discovered that it is the second least populated country in the world in relation to its size after Mongolia. I had actually been to Namibia once before back in 1982 nearly thirty years ago when as a very innocent and inexperienced traveller I had headed off alone to visit the said cousins. My Uncle Martin had come from Namibia to study in the College of Surgeons in Dublin back in the 1950s where he met my Aunt Rosemary, my Dad's sister. They married and returned to raise their family in Namibia where she lived all her life before she passed away after a short illness in early 2007. She returned to Ireland occasionally on family visits over the years but not as often as she would have liked as travelling was more difficult then and expensive. We were aware growing up of our Namibian first cousins but until then I had not had the opportunity to meet all of them. In 1982 I set off for three weeks to spend Christmas with the family and perhaps to see a little of the country as well. At the time it was an incredible experience and I was treated with kindness everywhere I went. I recall getting job offers from friends of the family and for a time I was really tempted to make a drastic lifestyle change and make a fresh start in Africa. I was only 23 at the time but realistically my own family would not have supported the idea. I had sporting commitments and ambitions that soon became more important and the idea of relocating to Africa faded after I returned home. But it was a fantastic opportunity at that age and definitely instilled in me a desire to travel and to perhaps return someday. In the following years our Namibian cousins had made the odd trip to Ireland and often encouraged us to visit them but until now it was never really possible. All these years later I was now planning to return with my own family and there was a feeling of great expectation and excitement as we counted down the days before our journey began. Our plans developed and our cousins were very encouraging and helped us to plan a mixed itinerary with something for everyone. We talked my Aunt Marie into joining us as well as it was such a good opportunity for her to visit the family. It was her sister Rosemary who had married and moved to Namibia all those years ago. Time passed quickly and our plans were well advanced when Marian and the boys finally got their school holidays in June. I had to wait longer for mine but it all added to the build up and our intended departure date on July 23rd.With the travelling party now confirmed at six and with a loose itinerary booked and mapped out there was only one slight snag to our plans. Two weeks before we were due to leave I received an e-mail from The Mokuti Lodge in the Northern area to say that our reservation for two nights in early August had to be cancelled due to an over booking. Although they were apologetic it left us with a major headache and little time to resolve it. Situated at the Eastern gate of the world famous Etosha National park the Mokuti lodge was going to be one of the highlights of our trip and now suddenly I had to make alternative plans. I quickly searched the internet and sourced some other lodges in the general area in order not to disappoint anyone and to fit in with the rest of the itinerary we had planned. Nothing jumped out at me and anywhere I tried was fully booked as this was high season and most of the popular lodges were choc o block! Then by chance I came across a small lodge situated in the Otavi mountain range called Guest Farm Ghaub. It was described as an historical working farm lodge with a unique atmosphere and as it was reasonably priced and located just ninety minutes from Etosha I decided to secure the booking and hope for the best. It was to prove to be a chance happening and a decision that would change all our lives in ways we could never have imagined.

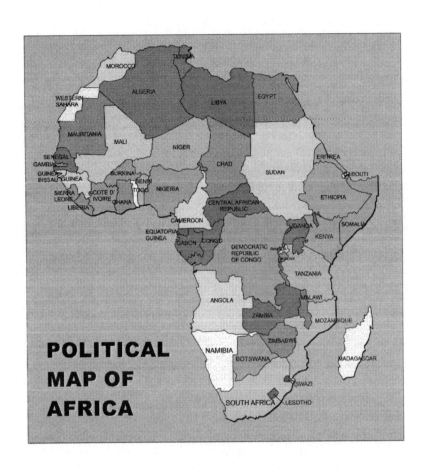

POLITICAL
MAP OF
AFRICA

THE TRIP

At last the day arrived and our eight seated taxi arrived on time to take us to the airport. I remember now the driver's name was Barry Cooney which was a good omen perhaps. I have never lost the sense of expectation when it comes to flying off on holiday and I actually usually enjoy the buzz of airports. Mind you I usually give myself loads of time to take the stress out of it and have been known to be sitting in departures for several hours before a flight. This was no different and we arrived in plenty of time for the first leg of our trip which would take us to Gatwick in London before linking up with the Air Namibia flight to Windhoek, Namibia pronounced Vindhook.We were all in the holiday mood and looking forward to the adventure ahead. Choosing the no frills option we had no complaints about the journey over to London and all our bags were accounted for. A swift transfer from the South terminal to the North terminal by train was efficient and easy to follow. So far so good. When it was time to pass through security we met our first hiccup. The queues were long and slow moving. There was no problem with the time but for Aunt Marie it was very tiring and I thought really unfair to keep people on their feet so long. But we got through eventually and were able to relax for a while over a light meal before the overnight flight to Africa. In total it takes ten hours but travelling through the night shortens the journey. Upon boarding the boys busied themselves with the various controls and free gifts while Marian and Marie made themselves comfortable. We then had another pleasant surprise when my cousin Martin happened to be flying the plane and promptly bumped the ladies up to business class. He also promised to give the boys a tour of the cockpit during the flight much to their delight. Martin is a very interesting guy and has been a pilot with Air Namibia for several years. He has incredible stories to tell of the places he has visited and you couldn't help notice how well respected he was by the crew. We were also planning to spend some time with him during our trip and he had in fact been very helpful in planning out our itinerary with us. The girls had a very relaxing journey while the lads were brought up to the cockpit as we flew in over Algeria and looked down on old oil wells burning from 30,000 feet with the flames shooting high into the night sky. It was a very spectacular sight and added to the magic of the occasion. The whole experience was magical flying in over the African coast at a speed of more than 600 miles per hour although it felt like we were barely moving at all. Martin explained the various controls to the lads and they were at their best behaviour. I was sure that we were experiencing a rare treat as in these times of tight security with the threat of terrorism it is highly irregular for passengers to be seen inside the cockpit of an international flight. I could see that even the crew were a little surprised to find us there huddled around the controls. As long as the Captain approved it seemed to be acceptable. We loved it and must have spent a good half hour there in total before returning to our seats. It wasn't easy to sleep after that but there was another treat for the younger members of the party in the morning when Martin invited them back up to the cockpit for the landing. Just the first of many magical experiences during a memorable journey. Disembarking shortly after 7.00am next morning we were instantly hit with a warm blast of African air even at that time of the day. The airport was small but had modern looking terminal buildings and efficient friendly staff. On the drive to Windhoek I am struck by the quality of the roads, the lack of traffic and the sense of space.

We stayed two nights with family in Windhoek and leaving Marie behind with the promise of linking up in a weeks time we headed off in our hired 4x4 Toyota Hilux across the gravel roads towards the Namib desert. It's just breathtaking and at first we find ourselves stopping every time we come across wild animals grazing by the roadside. We quickly realise that we will never reach our destination if we continue like this. Our journey takes us across rugged landscape which was always interesting. It's dry and sandy mostly and certainly not farming land. We are heading to a small place called Solitaire which is described in the guide books as an outpost that belongs to another time. They weren't joking and Solitaire is like an oasis in the wilderness and suitably named. Our only slight worry on route was negotiating a steep climb through the Ganesburgh pass when the driver pretended to be untroubled by the challenge of keeping the vehicle between the barriers when in reality he was more than a little concerned! We must have passed just about a half dozen cars in 300 Kilometres. You could be waiting a long time for help to come along in the event of a problem out here. They don't call it the big empty for nothing. We spent two nights at Solitaire which included a day trip to the famous dunes at Sossuslvei. It must be the eight wonder of the world and is almost impossible to describe. Considered to be set among the biggest sand dunes anywhere on earth Sossuslvei is one of the most popular attractions in Namibia. Ideally you should visit and climb the dunes at first light to experience the real magic of the place. It's just beautiful and for me it creates a sense of time and space that makes me appreciate how fortunate we are. Anyone coming to Namibia must see this place. We reluctantly move on from Solitaire the next day with a growing bag of memories and photographs that don't capture the beauty of what we have seen. I will never forget the late night walk we took behind the lodge through the desert under the stars which you could almost reach out and touch accompanied only by African night sounds of Geckos, owls and other unidentified creatures. Just magical. We travel over the Tropic of Capricorn, stopping off to capture the moment, towards the coastal town of Swakopmund through more gravel bumpy roads. It's again dry and desert like either side with just the occasional sighting of desert ostriches in the distance picking away at the scrub. It's hard to imagine how anything could survive out in this wilderness. We have arranged to stay at our Cousin Marie's summer house in Swakopmund and I remember the outline of the town from thirty years ago as we arrive from Walvis Bay. We spend five days in total at the sea and the boys have a ball. Swakopmund is where many white Namibians come to holiday and the architecture is obviously

German influenced. I am slowly beginning to learn more about Namibian history and the close connection between Germany and South West Africa as it was formerly called. We go quad biking in the dunes and at one stage we are surrounded by high dunes for as far as you can see. It's an incredible sight and again you get the feeling of the vastness of this wonderland. We also take in a day trip to see the seal colony at Cape Cross around an hour and a half northwards along the Skeleton coast. As we drive the landscape is lunar with miles of rock, scrub and sand as far as you can see. One can't help thinking that there are vast tracks of land that nobody has ever set foot on in Namibia. Our accommodation is very plush and we enjoy our few days by the seaside. Watching the sun disappear over the horizon in the late evening as we look out to sea is special. You see this big full orange ball sitting on top of the water and within minutes it disappears and plunges you into semi darkness. Yes this is a beautiful part of the world. We leave Swakopmund on a Sunday morning to travel north to our next destination. It is a five hour drive to Guest Farm Ghaub and the family are really looking forward to the next chapter in our journey. This is where the story really begins.

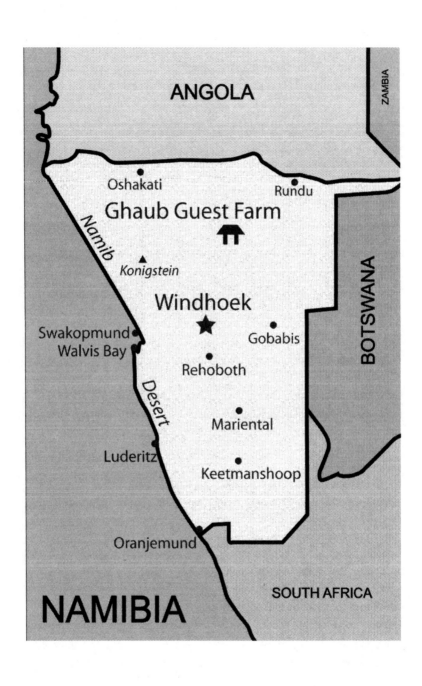

I

When you follow the path of your father, you learn to walk like him!

Ever had a longing? I have had one for years. It's hard to explain but I have always felt that there was something missing in my life even at the best of times. It's hard to describe but it felt like a restlessness or an itch that was impossible to reach. Even on holiday sometimes I would feel out of sorts and get bored easily. I would look forward to a break from work and then struggle to switch off when the time came. There are only so many books you can read, only so many hours you can sit in the sun or only so much swimming you can do. I would often throw myself into the gardening when I had a break and work like a lunatic for a few days. At least you could see the rewards for your efforts and there was some satisfaction in it. I could only switch off when I felt I had earned a break. Was it to do with the nature of the work I was doing as there is such intensity to it that it's difficult to leave it behind when you do take time off?

I have a very vivid memory from years ago back in 1991 when I went back to Trinity college to do Addiction studies as a mature student. In all honesty it came about really from a desire to take a break away from my job as a child care worker in Finglas Children's centre rather than a keen interest in addiction. But after I applied for this one year full time Diploma course I couldn't believe my luck to be given the go ahead to become a full time student on full pay for twelve months. Talk about landing on your feet! Trinity always held a special place in my heart and I dreamed of studying there at some stage of my life but never really believed it would happen. Now I was given

1

the chance to study something that I was interested in without any financial worries and with no end of year exams to worry about. It was perfect and I remember thinking this is as good as it gets. I again threw myself into the course with great enthusiasm and for the first term I was extremely content with my lot. But it didn't last and I started to become restless again. I tried to express myself at one of our weekly group meetings which I was finding difficult. Back then I had no experience of groups and struggled to appreciate what the purpose was and the facilitator's apparent reluctance to explain it. Anyway I remember declaring one morning in a rare moment of self disclosure that I still hadn't found what I was looking for. Well the group found it hilarious and cracked up laughing and I was left wondering what I had said that was so funny. I felt affronted and angry that they were having a laugh at my expense and I was the only one not in on the joke. Eventually someone made some reference to the U2 song of the same title and suggested that I should try to express myself without using clichés. I just felt judged and ridiculed and after that kept my longings to myself. I did ultimately really enjoy the year and it definitely gave me a confidence I was lacking and a new ambition to stretch myself. I also realised that a change of job or circumstance will not bring long term contentment in itself. You bring your thoughts and struggles with you wherever you go and sometimes no matter how relieved you can be to leave something behind, the feeling won't last until you find a better place within yourself. As I discovered in later years and found myself offering as advice to others-we shouldn't look outwards for something that we can only find within! I was to have many such introspective moments during the following 18 months which honestly I would struggle to make sense of.

On becoming the person you want to become
I have also asked myself at different stages of my life who I really was and didn't always like the answers that I came up with. I have another vivid recollection of a particularly signifi-

cant moment in my life when I was on a counselling course back in the early nineties. We were given a written exercise to complete titled "Who am I"? Up until then I had never really considered that question. I proceeded to write a list of my sporting achievements as I believed that was how my life was defined until that point. I handed in my work expecting the tutor to be impressed with my collection of medals and awards considering my less than obvious talents. Big mistake! She absolutely rubbished my attempt and told me in no uncertain terms to repeat it and this time she didn't want to hear anything about my sporting achievements. "I couldn't care less if you have run a marathon in less than three and a half hours, have won some medals and got your golf handicap down to four at one stage", she stated. She was only interested in who I was as a person and what was important to me. I was shocked and it really got me thinking. Until then I suppose I had defined myself by what I had done on the sports field and making the most out of a little bit of ability by training hard and looking after myself. I think it came down to a number of factors. School was always a struggle and I always felt under pressure to keep up with my peers. In fact I have always carried the feeling of being a couple of years behind everyone else growing up. At thirteen I felt out of my depth and unable to find my place socially with other guys my age. This followed me right through secondary school and I never quite caught up. As such it was always a battle to survive and the only way I could express myself was through sport where I could compete as an equal and maybe a little better than most. In hindsight I think it was as a result of both a sheltered upbringing partly and a lack of maturity. I now appreciate the importance of the impressionable years for any youngster from nine to sixteen yrs. For me these years were a real struggle as I was bullied in national school and had no ability to deflect unwanted attention. I didn't cope with it very well and like most young people faced with this situation I kept it to myself. I wasn't able to tell anyone and began to feign illness to avoid going to school. It got so bad that I actually developed severe stomach pains that I now can only guess was a result of extreme anxiety. My parents had me examined and the Doctors were at a loss and could only suggest a form of muscular fibrositis which lasted on and off for about two years. My secret remained a secret until eventually my Dad suspected something wasn't right at school and the head teacher was contacted and I reluctantly fessed up to what was going on. When you look back it's hard to appreciate what was so awful about it but I do remember feeling terrified of one guy particularly who took great delight in seeing me fall apart when he threatened me in front of his friends who seemed so old and intimidating but in fact were only a couple of years older than I was. Although the situation improved I now believe I began to fall behind emotionally as well as academically which was exacerbated when I was packed off to boarding school at twelve years of age against my wishes. All the family had gone to the same boarding school and I had no choice but to follow. I was under pressure straight away as much to my parents displeasure I was placed in what was considered the B class after a poor entrance exam. I am still convinced that they used their influence to have me bumped up after the first term exams when under pressure my grades improved and I was promptly moved in with the higher achievers. It meant that I was moved away from the friends where I was comfortable and put in the A class with the guys who were operating at a higher level. This wasn't easy at age twelve when I was already struggling to find my place. This was to become a pattern in my life as my parents on several subsequent occasions tried to influence the direction I was taking. It may have been well intentioned but just maybe it was more to do with not letting the side down but I grew to detest the interference and pleaded to be allowed make my own mistakes. Exams became a nightmare and I felt really stupid at times. Maths and Science became impossible and basic Irish was beyond me. I faced class most days in dread knowing that I wouldn't be able to recite two simple verses of an Irish poem if asked. What was so difficult about learning two easy verses I just can't figure? I recall getting called up to the board to explain a Geometry theorem and been ridiculed by the teacher in front of the class who were probably just relieved that they weren't picked. Another clear memory concerns having an English composition read out to the class by a teacher as an example how not to do it. We had been asked as fourteen year olds to write about a building that meant something important to us growing up. I chose an old building where we played as kids in Ardee which happened to be an old workhouse many years ago during famine times. It was a magical place to hang around as youngsters and I had lots of good memories of Saturdays spent there with friends. This so called developer of young impressionable minds made a laugh of choosing a workhouse as a special building because it represented past horrors of a depressing time in Irish history. I wasn't able to stand my ground or able to find my voice to defend myself. But deep down I knew he was the one missing the point. Amazing that it's still such a vivid memory. The only relief came for me on the football field or the handball alley when I could at least hold my own. However instead of winning approval because of my sporting ability I began to attract a hostile response from one or two people who thought I was showing off. I again was bullied and began to feel that I must have been walking around with a sign over my head inviting others to have a pop! It got so bad that my ability was resented and I deliberately under performed in games rather than stand out from the crowd. Not easy for a young person to do when struggling for affirmation in other areas. It took me many years to figure it out and it affected me greatly for a long time afterwards. I have since met some of my class mates at school reunions and was surprised to hear their reactions as most of them remembered me as a happy go lucky guy that they used to envy and look up to because I was sporty. They had no idea that I was just about surviving and had such a difficult time in school. In truth it took me many years to get over my experiences and I honestly received many hours of help before I learned to move on. Most of my anger was with myself for allowing it to happen. I believe now that most victims struggle as much with self loathing as much as anger towards those who hurt them. I had to learn in time to move on. The one consolation is that even though we are shaped by our experiences growing up if you reach a point of liking the person you have become then somehow it's easier to accept the hard times. For many years I remained behind myself emotionally and in a strange way the experiences I have had during my time in Africa have now allowed me to finally become the person that I wanted to become.

Return to the story

I remember vividly that long journey we took on that Sunday in early August 2007 travelling North East and marvelling once again at the landscape and surroundings as we passed. In all it took us more than five hours but we passed the time easily and in good spirits. A few short pit stops for cool drinks made the journey easier and we eventually pulled in to Guest Farm Ghaub mid afternoon. First impressions are always important and this felt homely and welcoming with an old world atmosphere. We were met with a smile and a welcome drink by Mika the local manager of the lodge. He brought us for a short tour of the grounds and we found our way to the hide just below the swimming pool where animals can be viewed in the evening at the nearby waterhole. We watched enthralled as right on cue just as Mika had predicted we could see several large Kudu appear from the bush as they inched their way across the open plain towards the water. This was the Africa we were expecting and wild animals in their own habitat carefully keeping to their ritual while obviously watching out for danger or other predators. We had to remain extremely quiet as the hide was only thirty or so yards from the water hole and the slightest movement could spook the Kudu into running back to the bush. Then soon after followed a few warthogs scurrying across the grass and mingling with the Kudu as they also stopped for a refreshing drink. Obviously neither poses a threat to the other and we watch them in awe. Mika later shows us to our rooms which are spacious and spotless and situated in a beautiful setting facing the mountains. Ghaub has made quite an impression on us and I am particularly smitten with the place. We later enjoy our meal and again Mika is serving us with kindness and courtesy. He seems to be doing everything and we jokingly ask him is he also the cook! We have an early night as we plan to leave early the next morning for a day trip to the Etosha National park which is an easy ninety minute drive from the lodge. Mika promises to supply us with a packed lunch and a guide book for Etosha and we are really overwhelmed with the reception we have had and the kindness of the staff. The following day was not disappointing and we see so many animals during the course of several hours in the Park. Etosha is one of the biggest National parks in the whole of Africa and attracts thousands of visitors daily all year round. The highlight for us was coming across a large herd of Elephant taking over a waterhole just as we arrived and sending a mix of Giraffe, Springbok and Zebra rushing off in different directions for their own safety. There must have been thirty or so in the troop including some little ones and they took over the waterhole for a half hour as they drank and bathed and rolled in the mud not twenty five metres from where we were parked. It was quite a sight and we managed to get some great pictures before moving on. We were later told how lucky we were as coming across such a large troop of Elephants is quite rare even in Etosha. The park is so big you can easily get lost and signage needs some work. But we managed to see so many species and had a magical first visit to Etosha. I have since returned many times and each time brings a different surprise. I would gladly visit every week if possible. We headed back for a late evening pre dinner swim and the temperatures remained warm despite the fact that this was supposed to be winter in Namibia. We again enjoyed the home cooking on offer and sampled more of the Ghaub hospitality. Mika explained the history of the lodge to us and how he came to work there. It was very interesting and just made the visit more complete. We were wishing that we had more time here but had planned to leave the following morning early. Unusually I was up at first light next day and Marian joined me for a walk as the sun came up. I just didn't want to waste a second of our time there. It was just heavenly and we watched various animals feeding and listened to the cries of the birds as they went about their business. I was just blown away by the place and was overcome by a deep sense of absolute peace which I struggled to express. I started to chat with Mika some more while the family were packing after breakfast and was just trying to describe how beautiful the place was and to thank him for his hospitality. I remember saying to him that I could stay here forever. I will also never forget his reply. He mentioned that the lodge and farm was actually for sale and that it would be possible for a European to buy the place as long as he had a Namibian partner. By Namibian law it is only possible for a foreigner to buy land in Namibia if he has a local partner who owns 51% of the property. This is quite common world wide as most countries insist on a similar arrangement to prevent large tracks of land or farms been sold to overseas investors for purely financial gain while adding nothing to the local economy. When Mika told me the price of the property it sounded like a lot of money but not as much as I would have expected considering what was involved. The owners would only sell the farm and lodge together and the price included all the stock, all the machinery on the farm and the lodge in total including every knife and fork. I did begin to think that this might be possible but just kept it to myself for the moment but I was definitely distracted as we drove off on the next leg of our long journey. We were keeping in touch with Aunt Marie regularly by phone and she also seemed to be enjoying her holiday. We were planning to link up with her in a few days and to catch up with all her news and to share our adventures. We spent the next few days with my cousin Andre and his family at his farm near Okahandja which gave us another memorable experience of life in Africa. I mentioned the lodge to Andre and we joked about the possibility of buying the property but in all honesty I did not believe anything would come of it and Andre too seemed unsure about the idea. We had a couple of days at Mount Etjo lodge before joining up with Aunt Marie in Windhoek. Mount Etjo is one of the most popular lodges with Europeans as the accommodation is first rate and they have stocked the enclosures with most of the big game animals that visitors want to see. Some people think it is a bit too much like a Zoo and overstocked but if you want to see animals then it is one of the places to consider on a trip to Namibia. Our last two nights are enjoyable in Windhoek and it just puts the cream on a fantastic memorable trip in a breathtakingly beautiful part of the world. Our hosts have been so kind and we have got to know our African cousins much better. I like to think that they have also discovered more about Ireland and Irish ways. The boys have loved the trip with many highlights and Marian has also been taken by the charms of Namibia. For Dad something has happened that runs deeper and I return home with lots to ponder and thoughts of just perhaps returning again someday-maybe soon! There has been twenty five years between my two visits to date to Namibia. How long will it be before the next visit? Will it be another lost opportunity or another what might have been? Whatever happens I just have an inkling that Guest Farm Ghaub found us as much as we found it and somehow I knew that I would see it again.

CHAPTER 2

BACK TO REALITY

We returned to Ireland in mid August and I returned to work the following week feeling just a little distracted. I have been working as an Addiction counsellor for the previous thirteen years in The Rutland Centre in Knocklyon on Dublin's south side. The Rutland is an incredible place and has become such an important part of my working life and personal development. I arrived in 1995 after working as a Child Care Worker in various settings for the previous sixteen years. Beginning in Sandymount I started in Park Avenue with the Sisters of Charity in 1979. Good times and fond memories before I moved to St Michael's House where I stayed for four years working with young adults with special needs. Again for the most part it was a rewarding time in my life and I did meet my wife Marian there. I remember clearly meeting her for the first time and thinking that we could end up together. Never believed in love at first sight until then. I moved on to Finglas Children's centre for nine years where I worked as a child care worker with youngsters who were sent from the Juvenile courts for assessment. Again mostly I have fond memories of my days there although there were challenging times I relied on the support of some of my colleagues and have made lasting friendships from our days in the trenches as we battled to survive in trying circumstances. You needed a sense of humour at times to keep sane. It was around this time that I think I developed as a coping mechanism a warped sense of fun which has remained with me today. I tend to see the lighter side of most situations and been able to laugh at myself and life challenges has been an important weapon in my armoury in recent years. I applied for a job as an Addiction counsellor in the Rutland after my stint in Trinity but in all honesty I wasn't prepared for

11

the work involved. At the time I was relieved to finish in Finglas as the job was changing and becoming more challenging and I wasn't sure I could keep going much longer. It was stressful and demanding dealing with difficult troubled youngsters who were more victims than villains themselves. Anything would have been better and I was thrilled to be offered a fresh start and a new career and a new challenge. I was to discover quickly that these were not good reasons to take on such a responsible position. I realised soon that I didn't have the experience or the skills required for the job and reached another crisis point in my life. I described it once as if I was been asked to perform an operation without even been to med school. I bluffed my way for four months hoping that I might catch up or pick up the skills from my colleagues but should have known that it would never happen and eventually had to hold my hands up and admit I was out of my depth. Like a swan I was gliding gracefully along the top of the water while my feet were going like the clappers underneath! It got so bad I nearly went back to my old job in Finglas. If I had I would never have raised my head over the parapet again and I believe I would have probably ended up becoming cynical and angry with the world. I was given a chance by my boss to gain the experience by moving sideways into the assessment department for six months. I ended up staying there for more than ten years which suited me and the organization. I have subsequently spent many happy years there and shared special times with some great dedicated people. My youngest son Gareth was born while I was working in the Rutland and I also experienced the loss of both my parents during my time there when the support of my colleagues was much appreciated. I would like to think I have friends there that I will always keep in touch with and have learned more from the people that have passed through the centre during my time there than I could ever give in return.

I returned to work refreshed and eager to share my holiday experiences in Namibia in August. The photos only went so far but I was enthusiastic about the country as a holiday destination and encouraged friends to consider travelling there sometime in the future. The memories of Ghaub particularly remained and I could not stop thinking about our time there. I began to do the maths and wonder could it be possible to buy this incredible place and make what could be a life changing decision. There and then I decided to think about it for a month and consider it from all angles. It would mean taking a significant financial risk. It would also mean taking time away from the family if I was going to set up this business. It would also mean taking time off work and applying for leave of absence. The more I thought about it the more possible it became but I also knew that a lot would depend on convincing my Namibian cousin Andre to get on board. I would need his farming expertise and of course it couldn't happen without having him as a Namibian citizen getting involved to satisfy Namibian law. As already mentioned and as in many countries local law insists that any purchase of land in Namibia must include a Namibian citizen who owns 51% of the property and overseas investors may own only the minority share holding. I waited until September 18th which is etched in my mind forever as I knew Andre and his wife Marlize were expecting their second child on that day. I wanted to make sure everything went well before sharing my thoughts and when I heard that Marlize gave birth to a healthy baby boy and Liam now had a little healthy brother Aidan I decided then to contact Andre straight away. Time was against us as I was aware that there was a lot of interest in the farm locally. I was keeping in touch with Mika and he was telling me of visits from prospective buyers. I asked Andre to just visit the farm and to assess its potential. He really wasn't sure as he had never heard of Guest Farm Ghaub and as a Namibian citizen he was aware of most of the leading lodges dotted around the country. Just look at it I pleaded and if it held no interest to him then all it would mean would be just the loss of a half day. Andre is constantly busy and I now realise that it would have been easy for him to decline but he did decide to visit Ghaub. Two weeks after Aidan was born he drove to the farm on his way back from Swakopmund where he was visiting his Dad, Uncle Martin. I waited impatiently to hear of his impressions of the lodge and farm. Would he agree to get involved and would he see it as a worthwhile venture? I knew it would have to suit him and he would need to see the potential in the farm and the lodge before committing. Andre is a shrewd business man and family connection or sentiment would not influence his decision. He e-mailed me two days later with a lengthy assessment of his findings. Overall he was extremely enthusiastic about his first impressions of Guest Farm Ghaub and the potential of the lodge. In great detail he outlined the strengths and weaknesses having looked carefully at the facility and spoken to all the staff. He believed the farm was not realising its full potential and the lodge could in time become one of the leading lodges in northern Namibia. I was delighted and it looked like the dream could become a reality but there was still much to do and time was precious. Because there were other interested parties in buying the property we needed to raise 10% of the purchase price within four weeks to secure first option on the farm. Then we would have to raise the balance within six weeks or else forfeit the deposit and lose the opportunity. It was a crazy time in hindsight as I felt so passionate about this place and was terrified of losing it unless we acted quickly. I had several problems to consider. I had no farming background, no experience in the service industry, no marketing know how and besides all that no money to buy the place! Yet I felt that this was going to happen and that I would be spending a significant period of time in Africa over the next couple of years.

I spoke to Marian first. She has always been incredibly supportive but this was different and would have serious implications for the family if it became a reality. I was proposing to borrow a large amount of money and also suggesting taking leave of absence from my safe pensionable job as an addiction counsellor to go to Namibia to manage the lodge and set up the business with Andre. Taking leave of my senses perhaps! I was planning to come home for two weeks every three months and hoping that Marian and the boys would come to Africa for at least a month during the school holidays. It was a business venture and a chance to secure our future. I was already think-

ing we might relocate down the line when the boys were finished school. Several people have asked me since how did your
wife ever agree to this? All I could say in response was that you
would have to meet her. Even friends were intrigued at the idea
and perhaps just a little envious. I think once we were not taking a huge financial risk and the business looked solid Marian
supported me and her encouragement meant that I could really
now begin to make serious plans. She would have to carry the
bulk of the responsibility looking after the boys as well as holding down a full time demanding job. My employers were also
extremely supportive and it was also very reassuring to know
that I had a job to return to if everything collapsed and the
plan backfired. Timing is always important in everything you
do and little did I know when making this major decision that
there was a recession coming around the corner. Looking back
now I realise that this would never have happened if we had
found the farm and lodge twelve months or even six months
after we did. So much changed in the following year with the
economic situation worldwide and Ireland suffered more than
most that there is no way I could have borrowed the money I
did or encouraged others to get involved. Again it was either
fate or good fortune depending on your point of view although
I struggled with it and felt the responsibility that I was taking
on as I convinced friends and family to share the risk and the
adventure with me. I realised that I would need backers as I
could never raise the purchase price myself and imagined that I
would need to bring on board investors who preferably would
have a farming background and could bring both financial and
agricultural assistance to the project. I thought I had the ideal
partner in my friend Kevin Kilmurray as we had become quite
close in recent years through our mutual desire to improve the
fortunes of the Offaly Senior footballers. That's another story
I suppose but Kevin apart from being a former GAA All Star
has an affinity with the land and a farming background which
offered a wealth of experience to me as well as good friends
in business who I thought just might be interested in getting
involved in this project. We arranged to meet and his associates

were taken I think by the idea of getting involved in a farm in Africa as it represented a different challenge and they were definitely interested. They agreed there and then that they would consider taking a share if Kevin could visit the farm and assess the potential as a venture and guarantee that their possible investment would not disappear into a big dark hole in the wilds of Africa. Based on his findings they would then decide to invest which I agreed to and the plan developed another stage. Meanwhile I was liaising with Andre on a daily business by e-mail and trying to focus on my job at the same time as no definite decisions had yet been made. There were some restless nights as although the plan was still in place there were many pitfalls and potential landmines that could scupper the dream. Anyway I booked two tickets to return to Namibia with Kevin and arranged a five day hop back over for early November to view the farm and lodge with him and also arranged for Andre to join us. Kevin is another workaholic that I knew if I left it up to him to decide the dates it would probably never happen. So I just chose the time, booked the flights and told him he was coming! Part of me didn't believe it until I met him early at the airport that Friday morning looking suitably dressed as always and we headed off to Gatwick on the first leg of what was now becoming a familiar journey! I had a few doubts. What if the place was disappointing this time? What if Kevin was unimpressed and felt unable to get involved or recommend it to his friends. I shouldn't have worried. I immediately knew upon driving back into the lodge that I was home and Kevin was blown away by the country in general and the potential of the farm particularly. We enjoyed walking and driving around the property for two days with Andre and there seemed to be a mutual respect between them and an agreed estimation that the farm could be improved and expanded in several areas. We spoke to the farm manager and he also impressed us with both his knowledge and his dedication to the farm. Billy and his wife Judith are German Namibian and have lived and managed the farm at Ghaub for fifteen years. They were hopeful that these new potential owners would re-employ them and allow them to continue their love affair with Ghaub. Billy has put his stamp on the farm and has developed a reputation as one of the leading maize farmers in this part of Namibia who is also more than capable with cattle and other livestock. We were all impressed and considered Billy to be an important asset to the project. Meanwhile at the lodge Mika was again his usual hospitable self and we were warmly greeted and introduced to all the staff. It was a whistle stop tour really and included a meeting with bankers and solicitors in Windhoek to ensure bank guarantees and to receive assurances that money invested would be safe in order to reassure the Irish partners. Things were gathering apace and most importantly Kevin was more than happy with the visit and could now appreciate why I was so enthusiastic about the country. On our return we met the potential interested parties and I spent the next three weeks trying to pull the whole deal together. It wasn't easy and I thought more than once that we would lose out as the figures were not adding up and although there was enthusiasm about the venture it was another matter to put the purchase price together. At this stage I had arranged the deposit myself with help from the family and it was touch and go as the deadline came closer. Andre was putting pressure on me from the Namibian side and naturally everyone on the Irish side wanted reassurances that their investment would not be lost forever. I have to say my family were great at this time led my sister Evelyn who rallied the clan and drove the deal through in the finish. We signed on December 1st 2007 and we were now co-owners and had a 49% stake in an 11,800 hectare African farm with a substantial cattle herd and a ten twin room lodge facility which was the envy of the tourist trade. I was ecstatic that we had pulled it off and the sleepless nights were worth it. Now all I had to worry about was how I could arrange to take the time to go out to develop the lodge and to also support the work at the farm.

I immediately applied for twelve months leave from my job giving a months notice. I was given nothing but encouragement and my employers and my colleagues could not have been better about it. There was certainly some who were surprised at my decision but most were genuinely happy for me and were extremely kind with their good wishes and strong support. I was given an incredible send off by the staff who arranged a special early Christmas dinner to mark my last day in Rutland after nearly fourteen years. It was an emotional day for me as I have many close friends there and the experiences has shaped me into becoming more the person I want to become. I have found a confidence which I never had before and a voice that I struggled to have heard previously. Despite the early challenges when I could have walked away I now appreciate that this has been hugely important for my own personal development and sense of self. I have carried a feeling of huge admiration for my colleagues for their selfless dedication to their work and to their clients. I was always dedicated but I feared my lack of know how would find me out. It helped to be told that it was alright to be yourself and that you didn't have to try to impress anyone or be someone you are not. This has been a recurring theme in my life and I was finally beginning to catch up with myself so to speak.

I had to pinch myself to prove that this was really happening. The time flew and I made my third trip to the airport in four months on December 30th. This time would be different as I was going alone and would be away for eight weeks until the end of February 2008. I had decided I would come home for Gareth's confirmation on March 1st and although it seemed a long way off I imagined I could surely last that long. However nothing could have prepared me for that first spell of time away from the family. It was the toughest thing I have ever done and I have never really acknowledged until now how close I was to packing it all in and returning home. The first month particularly was the worst by far and I asked myself more than once what on earth was I after doing? I will try to explain exactly what happened and how it nearly drove me over the edge. I suppose even paradise needs to be shared with the people you love.

Don't take another mouthful until you have swallowed what's in your mouth!

I was a bit giddy as I took the flight from London on that evening alone feeling apprehensive but also on a bit of a high. I had decided I would like to spend the New Year in Namibia and welcome in January 1st 2008 in my new home. Disembarking from the plane in Windhoek and feeling that initial blast of heat once again that greets you lifted my spirits. My first problem was how to get to Ghaub 450 Kilometres away in the far north. I had half expected to be met by one of my cousins or a friend of the family who would whisk me off and make my arrival easier. But everyone seemed to be on holiday as this time of the year many Namibians are on vacation and head to Swakopmund to the seaside to escape the heat inland. This is the hottest time of the year and temperatures can reach the mid 30s and beyond sometimes. Anyway I decided to get a taxi into the city and take it from there. I picked the whitest looking guy for some reason and he turned out to be good company and helpful in my hour of need. He introduced himself as Dixon and I have met him many times since. He is what's called a baster or a mixed race Afrikaner who actually had very little English. I tried to explain that I needed to buy a local mobile phone and then figure out how I could get a lift to Otavi. Trains are not an option in Namibia and public transport generally is poor. Most people look for a 'hike' or a seat in one of the many minibuses that you can't help noticing on the outskirts of all towns and villages. The 'hike' system is very interesting and for a reasonable fee you can usually get a lift to your destination but the arrangement is fraught with difficulty. Firstly the busses are usually overcrowded and poorly maintained. Safety or rather the lack of it is an issue and you are really taking pot luck if you choose this option. The biggest problem is that you can never plan when your bus will leave or what time it will arrive at your destination. Seemingly when you enquire you will be promised a seat at an agreed price but no definite time of departure. Soon you will be told! However what the vendor or driver really means is he will leave when the bus is full of passengers only. It's a kind of a game as busses appear almost full but then you never know if those sitting in are actually making the journey or are friends of the driver. You can spend from 10.00am to 5.00pm sometimes waiting in the heat and then face a six hour drive in an overcrowded space in a vehicle that may or may not be insured with a driver who just might have a licence! This is the norm however and the local people just get on with it. It helps I suppose that time is different here and there is always a feeling of what's the rush anyway!

Dixon drove me to a phone store and helped pick out a reasonably priced basic local phone that would allow me make local calls and sent texts or sms's. I paid around N$500 or 50 Euro which would be similar to what you would expect to pay at home. I had the feeling that Dixon had done this before and just maybe he would be getting a cut for bringing me to that particular store. He then brought me to haggle with one of the minibus or Combi drivers but I didn't like the sound of it and declined to take up the offer of a lift. I was snookered and beginning to panic as I didn't want to hire a car or pay a fortune to reach my destination many kilometres away. I decided instead to strike a deal with Dixon himself and offered him too much to take me to Otavi but I wasn't in a strong position to bargain. We agreed on N$1,500 which considering he had already spent two hours with me that morning I reckoned was just about reasonable. Conversation was difficult with his limited knowledge of English and my non existent knowledge of Afrikaans. Everything was good! No matter what I asked the reply was 'It's good' in a strong clipped Afrikaans accent. I rang Mika and asked him to meet me at the petrol station in Otavi and at least I knew then I would welcome in the New Year at Ghaub. Typically Mika was waiting for us with a smile and Dixon turned around almost immediately to retrace the four hour drive back to Windhoek looking just a little too pleased with himself. I have met him a few times subsequently and usually remind him of how he took advantage of the naive Irish tourist all those months ago on his first day in Namibia.

As we arrived I had another of those what on earth have I done moments! Here I was in a strange country knowing very few people and after leaving my family 10,000 miles behind. I had no farming background and had never employed anyone in my life. My entire working career has been in the caring profession and I have always worked for a wage which usually didn't come close to compensating me for the work involved. You will never get rich as a counsellor or a child care worker but I suppose I was never motivated by money. My Aunt Marie often remarks how hopeless I am with money. I prefer to think that I don't worry about it too much. Once I have enough I try not to get too hung up about it. I never had lots but I never owed anybody money either and that has always been my guide. This was different however as I was now essentially taking on the responsibility of a large establishment with a staff of ten who worked fulltime at the lodge. Andre would manage the farm with Billy on hand and they would be responsible for the nine workers we employed there. I had been thinking about ways of improving the lodge from the first time I visited and particularly since my return visit with Kevin in November. But I would have to make it up as I went along and hoped to learn as much as I could as quickly as possible from Mika about the day to day duties as well as dealing with visitors and tour operators. I had a good coach and really I have come to appreciate Mika so much over the past year. He has become a close friend and colleague as much as an employee and I have learned so much from him. He is an incredible guy really and possibly the most important cog in the wheel at Ghaub. His story is fascinating and we have had many long conversations about how he arrived at Ghaub. Not very tall but well built the first thing that strikes you about Mika is his willing smile and his beautiful set of teeth. I notice many black people have excellent teeth which they look after very well. He is always immaculately turned out also and takes great pride in himself and in his appearance. He carries himself with a confidence which is one of his most endearing features. Mika arrived at Ghaub ten years ago looking for work as a gardener. He was then twenty years of age and came from his home in Ovambo land in the North West. With very few skills and only his own local language he had little to offer but the lodge manager at the time decided to give him a chance. Over the years through sheer hard work and a willingness to learn he worked his way up and was given more responsibility as he showed such promise. He eventually was asked to manage the lodge three years ago when the then manager decided to leave at short notice and the owners needed an immediate temp to fill in. Under difficult circumstances and with little support he managed to show how capable he was and established himself as a highly efficient, reliable and hard working manager and became the face of Guest Farm Ghaub. Now he speaks fluent English, Afrikaans and passable German. He is proficient in all the local languages also and is still trying to improve. He has a fantastic warm personality and a terrific manner in dealing with guests. We are lucky to have him and we hope he will stay at Ghaub for a long time to come. He has received a few offers to move within the industry but out of loyalty and a strong attachment to the place he has decided to commit himself long term. I hope to take him on a holiday to Ireland someday and introduce him to friends and to another culture. I know he would be fascinated and would make a big impression.

I was determined to make a success of this venture but that first month was extremely difficult. This was the off season for tourists and we had no guests at all on 14 nights during that first month of January. The staff went home at 3.30pm each day as they started at 7.00am and I was on my own for the rest of the evening. We had no television, an unreliable phone line and no internet. I felt very cut off and isolated and I began to wonder again what I had done. I tried to busy myself during the day becoming familiar with the tour operators and making small improvements where I could. But the evenings were long and lonely and there were some surprises and challenges to contend with also. On my second evening there, a snake wandered into the dining room as I sat alone having dinner. I thought this should be interesting and called Mika thinking he would be experienced in dealing with such an unexpected visitor and

I might learn something. However he was more terrified than I was and I watched him struggle with a long stick as he tried to encourage the snake outside but from a safe distance. Eventually I decided to have a go and cornered the snake outside at the veranda and managed to kill it. I asked Mika was it poisonous to be told that it was a highly dangerous Zebra snake that can spit venom at you which can be fatal if it gets into your eyes! Well now you tell me I thought! I was to have about four close encounters with snakes over the next six months but never felt in real danger and learned quickly that snakes are usually just as keen to avoid contact with humans. You would have to be very unlucky to have a problem with a snake although The Black Mamba snake is considered one of the most dangerous creatures in Namibia and I have read the odd report in the local papers of isolated attacks.

I kept a diary during the first month and am surprised now to read back over it and remember how difficult it was. Mika was incredible during this time and kept me sane when I missed my family terribly during that first month especially. The whole experience was quite challenging and my surroundings were still very strange. It certainly was nothing like an average day in south County Dublin! On the way to the room at night I would hear all sorts of strange sounds in the darkness and the insects seemed to get bigger by the day. Each night brought different types of bugs depending on the weather. Once I had what I called a visit from the SAS ants which arrived in droves at the windows of my room as the light was still on. They proceeded to shed their wings and then creep under the door in battalions. There were literally hundreds of them in the room and I went around like a lunatic swatting them and couldn't sleep until I had eliminated the whole colony. On another night there was a swarm of hard back small beetles that filled the room in an instant and gave off a pungent smell when you squashed them. After a while though I didn't even notice the bugs and was actually never bitten by anything in all my time there. I suppose you get used to them and most of the lodges have mosquito nets covering the beds in the rooms in order to make it more comfortable for guests.

I decided that I would write a monthly report back to friends and family just to update the partners as to how the business was going and to give people a flavour of what it was like in Africa. It began as a serious monthly summary of the challenges I was facing but then grew into a more light hearted review every few weeks which in some ways provided me with a reason to keep a diary of events. As the time passed my mood improved and accordingly the reports were lighter and seemed to track the personal journey I was on as much as telling the story. It's interesting now to look back at how the months evolved and how my spirits rose and sank sometimes within minutes.

Wisdom is like fire. People take it from others.

I never lost the sense that this was a special place from that first afternoon that we arrived at Ghaub. I was instantly taken by the sense of calm and history that filled the air and I was eager to discover more about the previous inhabitants and the founders of this unique place. There is a large sign on the entrance wall which reminds visitors that Ghaub was founded as a Rhenish Mission back in the late nineteenth century. I decided early to research the history thoroughly and over a period of weeks I was able to find more and more information about the lodge and it's interesting past. The following is a short synopsis which helps to capture and part explains why there is a special atmosphere that hangs in the air and immediate surrounds of the main buildings on the farm.

In 1895 The Rhenish Mission Society established a reserve for the Bergdamara and Hai/ om communities at the farm Ghaub. The aim was to settle the nomadic people of the area and to acquaint them with agriculture. The farm measured 9000 hectares and had large swampy areas. The missionary Kremer arrived at Ghaub in July 1895.

The work at Ghaub comprised two separate areas, mission work, centred on the school and the church, and secondly agriculture. Soon after the first buildings had been completed in 1897 the first persons were baptized in the church. During this time the palm trees that surround the lodge today and are considered to be among the tallest palms in Namibia and are an eye catching feature of the landscape were also planted by the missionaries.

Mr Wilhelm Detering was responsible for the agricultural development at Ghaub. He had been sent out by the Rhenish Mission Society from Germany and arrived in August 1901. One of his duties was to drain the swampy areas which were then prepared for the planting of Maize. In 1903 the farm house, which was built from clay bricks was completed. Soon the first cattle also arrived from Otjisazu, Okahandja and Otjimbingwe. At this time more that forty families made a living from the produce which they cultivated in their gardens at Ghaub. They also kept some livestock and were expected to pay a fee of two German marks in the form of ground rent. During the Herero war of 1904–05 Ghaub was destroyed and plundered. As a measure of protection the missionary Kremer and Mr Detering, together with their families, were evacuated to the fort at Grootfontein, where the missionary died of malaria in April 1904. In October 1904 a new start was made when the Deterings were allowed to return to Ghaub. During the following years Ghaub was rebuilt to become a major centre for agriculture and education. Trees such as Casuarenes, Mulberries and pepper trees were planted close to the swampy areas. In addition some banana and orange trees which yielded some precious fruit over the years were cultivated. The stones and rocks from the fields were gathered and used for building walls around the vegetable gardens. These walls remain today and certainly contribute significantly to the old world feeling as one walks the land. The old cemetery was also moved around this time to a new site on a hillock around two kilometres from the main house. Today the cemetery is a fascinating feature of the farm and German guests particularly are very moved by the aura and sense of history that remains there as they recognise some of the German surnames on the marked graves.

During the years 1906 to 1908 missionary work at Ghaub was continued by the missionary Ferdinand Lang. In May 1911 Dr Heinrich Vedder arrived at Ghaub to teach young evangelists and teachers. A school building which was erected served for adults in the morning, for children in the afternoon and as a clinic in the evenings. Dr Vedder soon learned the languages of the local communities which enabled him to teach the different tribes in their mother tongue. One of the aims was to reach out to the Hai/om and Damara communities who gradually settled at Ghaub.

In 1912 a second agriculturalist Mr Hermann Eickmeyer was sent to assist at Ghaub. For forty four years the Eickmeyers lived at Ganachaams which today is the main farm house where the farm manager and his family reside some six Kilometres north east of the lodge. After Mr Eickmeyer's death in 1956 his wife stayed on in the old school building at Ghaub.

In 1913 Dr Vedder discovered the famous cave at Ghaub. Apparently the entrance to the cave only emerged after the extremely wet rainy season of 1911/1912. Today the Ghaub cave has national treasure status and is considered a national monument. With more than two Kilometres of chambers and corridors it is listed in guide and travel books as the third biggest underground cave in Namibia.

Due to World War 1 all work at Ghaub came to a halt. In 1919 Dr Vedder was deported to Germany but he returned to Namibia after the war and continued his work at Okahandja. In 1920 an effort was made by the Rhenish Mission Society to sell Ghaub for £20,000. However the deal did not materialise and in 1922 Mr Detering was sent back to Ghaub. In 1925 the mission exchanged a portion of Ghaub, known as Ghaub West in return for the farm Khorab which belonged to the Tsumeb mine. Because Khorab was much bigger than Ghaub West, the Rhenish mission was paid £800 in addition. Ghaub now measured 12,000 hectares. During these times large tracks of land on the farm were swampy and malaria was common.

In 1932 karakul sheep were brought in to Ghaub on an experimental basis. However there is very little known information regarding what happened but it seems for some reason this experiment was not successful possibly due to the poor quality of the grazing. Meat and vegetables however were sold to the mine at Tsumeb around this time. In 1938 Wilhelm Detering's son Karl moved to Ghaub to assist his father. However his assistance was to be short-lived as he was sent to internment camp at Andalusia in South Africa in 1940. The years 1941 to 1943 were extremely dry years and the Ghaub maize fields did not yield any crops. The rainy season of 1944 was so wet that it was impossible to plant maize at all. This typifies the challenges farmers still face in Namibia today as the climate is quite extreme and difficult to predict long term. In 1945 Dr Wilhelm Detering died in Grootfontein but his remains were taken to the cemetery at Ghaub and his plot is centrally placed to this day.

During the following year the Rhenish Mission dispatched a number of farm managers to Ghaub. The first to arrive in 1950 was a Mr Wilhem Shuffner. He was followed by Mr Schutte in 1951. During the 1960s and 1970s Mr Gottfried Linde and his family acted as farm managers during later years and Mr Ernst Albat and his family who had started at Ganachaams in the 1960's managed the property. The old buildings at Ghaub were no longer occupied on a permanent basis and were only used during occasional seminars and conferences. They gradually fell into disrepair due to neglect and damage caused by termites.

In 1989 the company Ohlthaver and List bought the farm with the intention of turning it into a guest farm and lodge. Mr Volker Steinstrater and his wife were the first to restore Ghaub to its once glorious appearance. The original buildings were meticulously renovated and all new buildings were designed according to the same style, therefore retaining Ghaub's historic character. Mr Steinstrater deserves much credit for the present condition of the lodge and the immediate surroundings. His attention to detail and his ability to retain the original character of the buildings while extending the lodge demonstrates his creative abilities and sensitivity. Mr Hartmood Hellweg and his wife Judith also joined the Ghaub team in the early 1990's to manage the farm and they remain to this day. Hartmood

THE BEST TIME TO PLANT A TREE

or Billy as he is called has developed a reputation in Northern Namibia as a respected maize and cattle farmer who seems to have a unique gift and feel for the local climate and soil conditions. Mr Steinstrater moved to Swakopmund to set up his own furnishing business in 2003. Mika Shapwanale was handed the responsibility for managing the lodge on behalf of the Olthaver and List Company for two years before the property was sold once more to Mr Andre Compion from Okahandja, Mr Gerry Cooney and their Irish partners in December 2007.

I continued to pick up more and more information about the history of Ghaub over the following 15 months. The word Ghaub apparently is part Damara and part Bushman but is loosely translated from the Damara word meaning arrow. Ghaub with a click is named after the reeds which the Bushmen found in this area on the swampy land which were ideal for making arrows for hunting. In an amazing coincidence the symbol associated with the origins of the name Cooney also contains an arrow. Further evidence that this whole adventure was predestined perhaps.

3

BLIND BELIEF IS DANGEROUS

At the end of the first month in Ghaub I wrote the following. 'I have been here now for more than four weeks having arrived in Namibia on New Years Eve. So far it has been extremely challenging but very rewarding. Each day brings surprises and tests one's character and fortitude. Namibia is such a beautiful country and clearly the African culture is very different to life in Ireland. The people here are mostly friendly and welcoming and I have not encountered a negative reaction or any hint of hostility since I have been here. The weather is extremely warm but never unpleasant. We have had heavy rains but they are usually followed by warm sunny days with temperatures in the mid 20's. Ghaub is a special place and I discover something new almost every day. We are located four hours north of the capital Windhoek. Roads are tarred and of good quality. Traffic is light and driving is easy. We are situated 25 km off the Otavi Tsumeb road and you can reach the lodge on a good surface gravel road from the B1 main road. There is also a more scenic and slightly longer drive through Kombat which is off the Grootfontein road. Even the dirt roads have a reasonable surface although after heavy rains you have to be very careful. The lodge is essentially located within the Otavi, Tsumeb, Grootfontein triangle. Surrounded by mountains it is an absolutely beautiful setting. This area is considered to be the agricultural capital of Namibia because of the fertile land and the regular rainfall during the months of December, January and February. It is not unusual to have six months of dry, warm weather with not a drop of rain at all from April to October. This year the rains were later than usual and December was exceptionally dry. This has serious implications for the planting of the maize which is the main crop grown on the farm. Apparently there is a cut off date in mid January typically when you have to plant or risk losing your crop for the year due to a lack of water or at times too much at one time. Some of the farms locally have irrigation pivots and as such can control the amount of water the crops receive. This is expensive and the call for farmers is to weigh up the merits of a higher yield with irrigation against the added cost which can be prohibitive. Most farms rely on the rainfall and therefore predicting the fall of the first rain of the season is crucial. If you delay too long it is impossible to plant as you cannot get the heavy machinery into the fields. It seems that Billy, our farm manager, got it right this year. He waited while others panicked and he decided to plant on January 14th which I watched with interest. It was a painfully slow operation with old machinery and what appeared outdated methods but the rains came two days after the last of the seed was in the ground. Now after two weeks the maize is already appearing over the ground after daily rain and warm temperatures which are perfect growing conditions'.

During the planting I rambled up one evening from the lodge shortly before dark just to check how things were going and to lend my support. Billy asked me as a favour to collect some of the workers who were working at the perimeter fence at the North East side of the farm. Essentially it was a challenging drive over rough mountainy terrain which should take me about 30 minutes. Eager to be helpful I agreed although my limited knowledge of the land at that stage was going to test my sense of direction and my questionable ability to stay calm under pressure. It wasn't until I had travelled alone in the 30 year old Land Cruiser for about 20 minutes that I realised just what I had taken on. I hadn't a clue where I was going and could see the evening closing in fast. I managed to find my way over the first mountain by following the path but then the terrain became rougher and the path was difficult to find. There were a couple of forks on the road that was visible and I literally chanced my luck and chose one direction over the other more in hope. Just as I was starting to panic as I was completely lost I came across the boundary fence which I followed for another kilometre before I spotted a couple of guys waving their crude looking implements trying to attract my attention. There were five young lads in the work party and they were as relieved to see me as I was to see them. Even the journey back in semi darkness was eventful and I learned a valuable lesson. When in doubt speak up and ask for help.

At the lodge business is slow and we have a lot of work to do to market the facility and attract the tour operators. There are 10 twin rooms which are spacious and spotless but need a little attention. We are making small changes already and the staff are hard working, motivated, punctual and very positive. We have a staff meeting every Monday at 9.00am when we review the week just gone and plan for the week ahead. January is traditionally the quietest month apparently for visitors as most Namibians have returned to work after their 'summer' holidays and the Europeans do not travel in numbers at this time of the year. You get the odd couple who arrive without a booking who are just touring alone. They are often interesting seasoned travellers who prefer to do their own thing rather than rely on a guide to show them around. But overall it's quiet and if you consider bed occupancy of 20 beds for 31 nights a 100% occupancy would give you 620 nights for example. We have less than 60 guests for January or less than 10% occupancy which you could obviously not sustain for 12 months. However advance bookings are encouraging and July, September and October are strongly pre-booked at this stage. I am now getting used to my new surroundings and routine but I have to admit there are times when I am really struggling. I am missing the family hugely and the work seems endless. The evenings are the worst and I find the long nights really difficult. Cooking my own dinner is becoming the highlight of the evening as I ask the staff to work 7.00am to 3 30pm when we are not expecting guests in the evening. If we do get walk ins I can call down for the chef who will come in if needed. It means I don't see anyone from 3.30 pm until 7.00am the next morning several evenings and with no contact with the outside world I ask myself again what am I doing here!

I got stuck into Trevor Brennan's book 'Heart and Soul' which I enjoyed and the couple Of Ricky Gervais DVDs that I luckily brought with me. I was always interested in Trevor Brennan's rugby career and followed his chequered career from Barnhall to Wanderers and eventually to Toulouse in France. I have always been a sport fanatic and followed Irish teams particularly in all codes. I never played rugby but enjoyed watching it and particularly the stand out characters that always made an impression on games that they participated in. Trevor certainly made an impression on his opponents and the story goes that even in training nobody wanted to play against him as he played with the same intensity and ferocity even in practice. I could never understand why he didn't win more caps for Ireland as the French loved him and he was winning Heineken Cups for fun with Toulouse when he couldn't get a look in with Ireland. Anyway his book is a great read and I read one chapter every night at one stage to make it last longer and relived the matches he described in his own self depreciating way. I hope to meet him some day. I also relied on the few DVDS I had during that first month. I could recite most of the Office series and also Extras with English comic Ricky Gervais. He is an absolute genius comedian, actor and writer. I love again the self depreciating aspect to his comedy and his timing. I watch both DVDs several times and really they keep me sane at a time when I thought I was losing it. One consolation was that the guests we did have were extremely complimentary about their experience at Ghaub. The challenge seems to be in getting people here as the setting and facilities are as good as any other lodge in this part of the country. Marketing has been minimal for the past two years as the previous owners had clearly no real long term interest in the future of the lodge. We decide to drum up business by inviting two representatives from the ten leading Tour Operating companies in Namibia for a complimentary weekend in March. This will be a major undertaking and an opportunity to showcase the lodge to the most influential players in the tourism industry.

I speak to Andre and arrange some other meetings with the tour companies in Windhoek at the end of February. So far we have had mostly German, South Africans and Dutch people staying here. We try to find out as much information as possible from each visitor in order to improve the service and to know where to pitch our marketing efforts. The German market is clearly crucial and definitely needs to be prioritised. There is a holiday Trade Fair in Frankfurt in March which we may decide to attend. I am also busy trying to improve communications at the lodge as we need the use of the internet urgently and cell phone reception is only available at certain points around the farm. The staff know every spot where reception is strong and you can find a signal in the most unlikely of places. Our phone system needs attention and our fax machine can be temperamental too.

One of the frustrations I am experiencing is not been able to make the changes I would like sooner. I would love to introduce horses to the lodge and offer horse trails around the farm which some of the high profile lodges offer. We have all this room and guests do expect to have a choice of activities when they visit. I want to make Ghaub a destination in itself rather than an overnight stay which people visit on the way to Rundu, the Caprivi Strip (not a nightclub) or Etosha. I am getting into a good routine of rising at first light at 6.00am and working right through the morning. There are always jobs to be done and I have been trying to meet our neighbours and introduce myself locally. So far I have to say everyone has been very welcoming. I have been in the local towns shopping a few times and have never felt uncomfortable. It's a long day as I usually lock up around 10.00pm or whenever the last guest has retired for the night. I have been noticing the number of animals around the lodge and beginning to appreciate the wildlife in its natural habitat. It is not unusual to see herds of Kudu grazing nearby at different times of the day. The Kudu is a beautiful creature and member of the deer family with distinctive brown and white stripes. The males have large antlers and are noted for their ability to jump over high fences from a standing start. They would make great puissance jumpers if you could catch one. They scare easily though and are nervous by nature. There are also daily sightings of warthogs which are like wild boars like the Pumba character from the Lion King. They travel in packs and usually there are a number of little ones in each group. You tend to see their swishing tails first as they shuffle around picking at roots and shrubs. They also have a curious way of drinking water at the water hole by bending their front legs into a kneeling position. In the early mornings I sometimes have to chase baboons off the roof of the garage as they mooch for food. Something else you don't often see in Churchtown on an average morning!

I have just finished building a hen house with help from Immanuel and Lotto, two of the staff. I actually got a bad touch of sun burn when I became carelessly engrossed in the work forgetting momentarily that the sun can be extremely hot even early in the morning. There is a relaxed informality during the work and they impress me with their willingness to get stuck in and their ingenuity when it comes to creating a structure for the chickens from odds and ends. I am hoping to be supplying soon our own fresh eggs daily to our guests. I have also started to learn how to ride horses after a few failed attempts over the years. I have always had a keen interest in horses but never really had the opportunity to be around them. For now though I settle on borrowing one of horses belonging to the farm manager and his daughter offers to give me a few lessons. So far my biggest challenge is to keep the horse awake and interested as he is old and lazy and knows that I am only beginning. He pulls up if I don't keep him moving and only perks up when he is on his way home after exercise. I am missing home hugely still but slowly beginning to find my feet and determined to stick it out. I got myself a pup from the local pound in Tsumeb last week and he is already great company and follows me around everywhere. I decided to call him Bono as he has a bit of an attitude and I have been listening to a lot of U2 since I arrived. Hoping that friends at home will come out to visit and experience this incredible place.'

On reading back over this much later I am reminded of both the highs and lows of those first few weeks in Africa. I recall the nights when I had serious doubts about the whole venture and thought I had made a huge mistake. I just had to make it work as it would have been too difficult to have to admit to some people that maybe it wasn't such a good idea after all. I knew there were a few people who seriously questioned my sanity when they heard about it but it just made me more determined to prove that it was possible and a good investment. I thought I was over the worst of it and anyway my sister Evelyn and Aunt Marie would be coming out in a few weeks and that kept me going.

OUR DEEPEST FEAR

Our deepest fear is not that we are inadequate
Our deepest fear is that we are powerful beyond measure
It is our light, not our darkness that most frightens us, we ask
ourselves who am I to be brilliant, talented and fabulous,
Actually who are you not to be?
You are a child of God.
Your playing small doesn't serve the world.
There is nothing enlightened about shrinking so that other
people won't feel insecure around you.
We were born to make manifest the glory of God within us.
Its not just in some of us, it's in everyone and as we let
out light shine
We unconsciously give other people permission to do the same.
As we are liberated from our own fear our presence
automatically liberates others.

(Nelson Mandela-Inaugural speech 1994.)

This passage from the inaugural speech by Nelson Mandela always resonated with me. I like the sentiments and they stayed with me during the early months at Ghaub. I later discovered that the words are actually from a poem by writer Marianne Williamson. She has written some beautiful poems and stories which deserve greater acclaim. A good friend Barbara Egan introduced me to her work and I will always be grateful

At this stage I was growing into the challenge and was becoming aware of how I was beginning to change as a person and seeing things from a different perspective. I think it was the Namibian people and the staff especially that were having such an impact on me and influencing my outlook on life. I admired their attitude and their understated contentment with very little. Their acceptance of me into their world and their generosity of spirit restored something in me that had been lost in years of cynicism and distrust. It was a cultural thing but a powerful realisation hit me that we have lost our way at home and I had lost my own sense of what really matters. I had hardly ever met a black person before now apart from the occasional contact with foreign doctors and a few foreign students at the various courses I had attended over the years. I certainly never had a meaningful conversation with a black person before as in reality Ireland remains predominantly white despite the influx of foreigners into the country over the past twenty years. I was now forced into spending all my time with younger people mostly from a very different culture with different customs and beliefs. I would have considered myself to be open, non judgemental and accepting of all things different. I definitely would have believed in equality for all and equal rights of opportunity. Martin Luther King was a hero of mine and I have kept records of some of his most memorable speeches. I liked the informality that I met here when I arrived first and the fact that the local people neither looked up or down at me. I could take my place in the queue in any shop as the only white person with 100 black people and feel relaxed and at ease making small talk with strangers. I had read that Namibia was one of the African countries that worked and that since Independence in 1990 the country had prospered under their own black government and black police force. My initial impressions were that the country was safe, welcoming and all inclusive as there were many different cultures and tribes living and working peacefully together. Our staff at the lodge were a mix of Ovambo, Damara and

Kavango although at that stage I would have difficulty recognising the now obvious differences. I was soon informed that it was quite alright to ask someone what tribe they belonged to. I assumed wrongly that this might be a rude question to ask. In fact people are proud to talk about their origins and like to explain their own particular beliefs and traditions. We agreed to retain all the staff that had worked at the lodge under the previous owners. I wanted to get to know them quickly and reassure them that I would treat them fairly and always with respect. In return I would expect them to be honest and reliable and I would attempt to improve their conditions as much as I could. I decided to have a meeting every Monday morning when I arrived first and these meetings were proving to be helpful and good for morale. Any problems were dealt with immediately and I tried to affirm the work that was obviously been taken seriously. This was a new departure for me as I realised that I had never ever employed a person before as all my previous jobs were for organizations that you could loosely describe as belonging to the caring profession. I just made it up as I went along and relied on Mika to keep me in check and keeping the staff on my side. It wasn't difficult really as the staff created very few problems and there was a relaxed atmosphere mostly. When I did have to question something it was usually down to a lack of understanding rather than an unwillingness on their part. I suppose they knew who was the Boss but there was room for a joke and a laugh at times as well while getting the work done. I began to lighten up a little and was now more familiar with the challenges facing us and was full of enthusiasm and ideas. In hindsight I must have driven Mika mad with my impatience and eagerness to sort every little problem out immediately. February was a satisfying month and we made great strides in tackling the jobs identified. I wrote a lengthy newsy summary for the partners and friends at home as I tried to give people some idea of what life in Namibia was like. I was beginning to feel like a cross between Basil Fawlty, Indiana Jones and Frank Spencer all at once.

Again those accounts now take me back to the early stage of a personal journey that was proving to be challenging yet rewarding. 'After a slow start in January when it was very difficult to adapt to this challenge the last four weeks have been much better. Ghaub continues to change in appearance by the week and we are now looking out at green lush grass everywhere after the scorched dry ground that prevailed in January. The rain that started on the 16th of January has continued almost daily although temperatures have remained high which happens to be ideal growing conditions as you would imagine. The maize is looking healthy and strong in each field totalling around 160 Hectares. It is incredible to see it now three feet off the ground after only seven weeks since planting. Harvesting is anticipated in late July and generally takes six weeks to complete. Machinery is old and dated but well maintained and as there is no danger of rain in July the workers can take their time to complete the job properly. The grazing has improved too and the cattle now have plenty of fresh lush grass that is rich in nutrients. It shows in their condition and when driving through the camps you see healthy strong looking cattle that are clearly thriving. At the lodge business is still on the slow side as expected with February occupancy about the same as January running at just over 10%. However we are working on the marketing side and bookings are still coming in for later in the year. The guests we do have continue to be very positive in their feedback and our guest book is filling up with compliments from satisfied customers. We took delivery of a new John Deere Tractor mower two weeks ago and it now takes us one day to cut the lawns around the lodge instead of three. We have been busy painting outside and clearing up in readiness for the arrival of the tour operators that we have invited up in March. We have 14 confirmations so far from some of the leading players in the Namibian tourist industry which we hope will re-establish Guest Farm Ghaub as a desirable place to visit.'

Since my last report there have been a few major developments which I will explain. I met Andre in Windhoek on Wednesday February 6th and we had two very productive meetings. We first met a Mr Wimpie Van Vuurren who is the Senior International manager with Air Namibia. We discussed corporate rates and the possibility of offering special rates to Irish visitors coming to Namibia. He was very interested in the lodge and the whole Ghaub operation. He gave us assurances that we should receive up to 25 corporate flights annually at a significantly reduced price. It is our intention to make these flights available to the partners and immediate family members. We also had a meeting with a lady from Baraka marketing called Leonie Van Niekerk. Leonie is apparently one of the leading marketing people in the Namibian tourism industry who worked closely with Andre many years ago when they were both involved in Air Namibia. She represents several of the leading guest farms and lodges in the country and comes highly recommended. After a long discussion we offered her a monthly retainer to represent Ghaub and my experience in the business world moved on a notch! Leonie has good contacts in the trade and we are pleased we have made a good addition to the team. The other reason I had come down to Windhoek was to collect my sister Evelyn and Aunt Marie who were flying in on the 7th for two weeks. They stayed for five nights at the lodge before moving to Swakopmund to visit family and do a little sight seeing. We had an interesting event on the Sunday morning they were here after we decided to attend church locally in nearby Otavi. The previous evening at the lodge we had visitors from Grootfontein for dinner who introduced themselves as Hans and Isle and they had a charcoal business not far away. Over dinner we got chatting and Hans mentioned that he was also a preacher and invited us to church the following morning. So Evelyn, Marie and I headed off early next day in our old reliable Toyota. After a few enquiries we found the Dutch reform church we were looking for and it was an interesting experience and very different to anything we experienced before. Marie became quite animated at one stage and was clearly upset by something that she heard during the service. As the proceedings came to a conclusion she made what could only be described as a beeline for the preacher who was deep in conversation with an elderly gentleman. I tried to intercept her to remind her quickly that we were guests and visitors to their church and whatever upset her may have been unintended. Turned out that Marie had noticed that the large map of the world which was painted at the back of the altar in large colourful shapes did not include Ireland. She demanded an explanation and was reassured that there was no slight intended and so an international incident was avoided! We were invited to join the congregation for lunch afterwards and there was a feast provided for all in attendance. I don't think we will be reconverting but it was an interesting experience and another experience of life here.

I really enjoyed taking them around the farm and this certainly was the highlight of the month. I was beginning to feel at home here now and it was encouraging that Evelyn seemed to appreciate the magic of the place. The Irish partners who had invested in the business also arrived out in February for a short visit and we sat and planned the future direction of the farm particularly with Andre and Billy the farm manager. It was interesting to listen at the different views and how Irish farming methods compared to Namibian farming ideas. The general consensus seemed to be on the need for an aggressive attack on the encroaching bush to improve grazing for the cattle and to extend the acreage for the maize. They also discussed the best use of bailed hay which was looking good for this year and when the cattle should be bought and sold. All agreed that most of the heavy machinery on the farm was functional but dated and needed investment. Everyone seemed to be on the same wavelength and was enthused about the potential for expansion. The maize seemed to visibly grow during the week the partners were there. The grass fields are still lush and thick and look ready for cutting. The Irish 'branch' was in favouring of cutting grass immediately and then perhaps we could cut again in three months with the rapid growth rate. However the local opinion insisted that you shouldn't cut grass until after the rainy season is definitely finished and this remained a contentious issue. I couldn't offer an opinion but imagined that the

The Cooney and the Compion family at farm Elisenore

Quadbiking in the incredible dunes near Swakop

Gerry, Anthony and Andre with Namibian Tour Operators at Ghaub

Frieda and Ida and the Ghaub children bring their entries for the design a sign for the meditation room competition

Gerry and Alandri Compion take the horses for a canter

Ghaub United in their new Leinster Playstation Jersies

Ghaub Lodge in the early 1900's

You never know what might wander into the garden

A typical stunning Ghaub sunrise

Late evening scene near the waterhole on the farm

The staff react to seeing the sea for the first time
(spot the Offaly Jersey)

Himba ladies in Outjo

The Maria Bronn children enjoy their day at the lodge

Hard to believe that 150 children travelled to Ghaub in this cattle truck from the School

Martin on his trusty John Deere

Breda and Stephen Mc Cormack with the sisters and children

locals knew what worked here and trusted their judgement. It was a fruitful exercise and now it felt like we were really planning for the future and everyone was hoping to remain involved for the long term.

We have continued to make small improvements around the lodge as well. We now have our own cows which we milk every second day and no longer depend on getting our milk from the farm. We were even buying milk sometimes when I arrived here first which was daft. I bought some chickens during the month as well and hope to soon have our own free range eggs. You have to be careful however as the baboons and the mongoose have already shown an interest in them so they are locked in well before dark each evening. I always felt destined to keep chickens at some time in my life. I think it goes back to spending time as a youngster in Westmeath with my Uncle Dick and Auntie Clare Nangle and family during my school holidays. It was a magical time for a townie and I spent many happy times there. I was always most interested in the hens and bringing in the eggs. Now years later I was enjoying again country living and playing at being a farmer. I kind of knew it would happen but didn't know when or where. Things were taking shape and we were getting through the long list of things to do. It was around this time that I had the most amazing experience and one that would ultimately prove to be a defining moment during my sojourn in Africa. The Irish partners were planning to come out in late February and I wanted to show them some local attractions as well as making sure the lodge was looking it's best. In expectation of Pat and Padraig's arrival I enquired locally about a Roman Catholic service as I knew they were regular church goers and would appreciate the opportunity to attend an African service during their short stay. I had passed a school a few times on the way to Grootfontein to shop for the lodge and had a vague idea that it was a convent of sorts with English speaking nuns. I dropped in one Friday and there were what seemed like hundreds of black youngsters lining up for class in an orderly fashion. There were boys and girls and all looked like they were around 14 years of age and younger. I got some quizzical looks and obviously it was unusual for a white male to drop in out of the blue. I was welcomed however in a friendly manner and was directed to what looked like a staff room where there was three or four middle aged teachers having a break. I asked about a catholic Sunday service and was told that we would be welcome any Sunday at 9.00am for the weekly celebration. I was just grateful that I had found somewhere to bring the guys and maybe any future Irish guests who might be visiting. The following Sunday we headed off and were immediately struck by the amount of children queuing outside the church all dressed up in their Sunday best. We were greeted by some elderly nuns and encouraged to take our place at the back of the small church which was almost full. What followed during the next hour will stay with me forever. There were about 300 children, 30 or so nuns and about 20 others who looked like they lived close by. I was waiting for a priest to arrive but there was none and one of the nuns led the service and more or less said a full mass without a consecration. But it was the singing that blew us away! If you can imagine 300 little voices singing in harmony with passion and enthusiasm in their own native languages accompanied by home made drums played randomly by some of the children. It is almost impossible to describe. I remember looking out the window at one stage with the sun rays filtering in over a gentle breeze and listening to the incredible sounds that filled the place and thinking this is magical and I should hold on to the memory. There were also some English songs with the emphasis on certain words as only Africans pronounce which brings a smile to my face. I look over at the two lads with me and we shake our heads in awe at the moment. The nuns made a fuss of us later and could not have been more welcoming. They explain the history of the Maria Bronn School and seem to be genuinely enthused about their work. I am struck by the relaxed atmosphere here and the fact that the children seem very happy and at ease. I discover that they are all from poor families from the surrounding areas and they board at the school from six to fourteen years before they graduate to senior school or Secondary as we know it. The children attend school where everything is taught through English although they keep up all their own particular tribal customs and languages. The nuns are part of the Benedictine order and all Namibian, black and proud! I am just blown away by the experience and promise to return.

Subsequently I have returned to the Maria Bronn School as often as possible and have developed a close friendship with the sisters and many of the children. I have brought friends and guests to witness the service at every opportunity and have looked forward to going back each time. In fact it has restored my faith in ways and has greatly enhanced this whole experience for me. I had become cynical, disillusioned and sceptical regarding recent revelations in the church and felt let down in ways. I had held on to my beliefs and continued attending church regularly when friends were moving away in droves. I wanted to remain committed but it was becoming more difficult and was struggling trying to pass on something that had been passed on to me. I believed it was my duty to encourage my kids to attend weekly service until they were old enough to make up their own minds. But it was getting harder as I was losing my faith in people largely because of recent scandals and the church's insistence on covering up for the wrongdoings of its members. But my experience at this extraordinary school rekindled something in me that I had lost. I believe now it was two things particularly. Firstly the selfless dedication of the nuns combined with their humility and generosity of spirit which was striking. It was obvious to me that the sisters were very comfortable with their vocation and had a calm sense of serenity. The Sunday service felt like a real celebration and nobody seemed to be there unwillingly. Secondly it was the children that won me over with their infectious enthusiasm. They showed such passion and pride in what they were doing. No inhibitions whatever and there was no sense of routine or ritual. Those who were chosen to read did so with pride and confidence. They marched proudly to the front on cue and always looked relaxed and assured. It was as if they were saying "this is my turn today, I am happy to be chosen and I am going to give it my best shot". Everyone sang out the words with emphasis and often moved and swayed to the rhythms. It was the older boys that struck me most forcibly with their energy and freedom as they expressed themselves with absolute devotion and abandon. I loved it and kept going back to experience it again and again. I enjoyed the reaction of the guests I brought along who were curious to witness another side of Namibian life too. For me it became the highlight of my week when I came away feeling energised and full of appreciation. I had many such moments of contentment when my life was put in perspective and I contemplated the meaning of real serenity. We are all shaped by our early experiences and a basic need to be loved and to feel safe. Without that there is always something missing and through my work over the years in addiction I now understand that lots of people attempt to fill that need with alcohol, drugs, food and gambling or whatever takes them away from themselves. What motivates people to act out is often a deep wanting and desire for something that seems unattainable through natural, conventional, acceptable pursuits. The promise of a temporary high or momentary escape is hard to refuse sometimes but ultimately proves dissatisfying. I believe it's motivated by the desire to fill a void or a hole in the soul as some describe it. For me the children of the Maria Bronn school in Grootfontein are inspirational and they have given me far more than anything I have given back in return. I hope to remain closely involved and look forward to sharing the gift with more and more Irish and European friends. I felt many times that this was a spiritual journey I was on as much as a business venture. I almost felt like a missionary at times but not in a religious sense. Even though I was now living among people from a very different culture and background I was realising that we were really not that different. Kindness is universal and overcomes barriers. A smile is a smile in any language and offers assurance in unfamiliar surroundings. Just maybe I am catching up and slowly becoming the person I wanted to be.

We were busy getting the lodge ready for the arrival of the Tour operators for the complimentary week-end. I wanted to introduce an Irish element and was becoming aware that I was wearing my Irishness on my sleeve. Whatever it is about working abroad but something seems to heighten one's sense of where they belong. I was certainly conscious that I was trying to hold on to all things Irish. I would go on to read many Irish books, listen to Irish music and introduce the country to many people who never heard of the Emerald Isle. We have a lovely quiet meditation type room in the garden at the lodge that was built by a previous manager. It's got a unique atmosphere and I started to spend some time there when I wanted to get away for a few minutes alone. As soon as you step into it you can switch off and allow your imagination to run wild. I wanted to turn it into a special quiet space that guests could also enjoy which would add something to their experience. I decided to name it the Ciunas room after the Irish word for quietness. In order to involve the staff and their families I had a competition and offered a prize for the best ciunas sign which I promised to hang up in the room. I didn't really expect much of a response but as it happened there were several entries and there was clearly a lot of effort and thought put into it. I announced the final date for all entries and we had an assortment of homemade shapes on different materials picked up around the farm with Ciunas clearly written and spelt correctly somehow on each entry. I got a great kick out of the effort that was put into it and many of the children of the staff arrived on the day with their carefully put together signs in hope of a prize. We gathered in the Ciunas room for the unveiling and I had to make a speech and get a bit of mileage from it. It was impossible to pick a winner without disappointing the majority so I kept all the signs and declared them all winners and we shared out the prizes. Even the adults were obviously pleased with themselves. We now have a Ciunas room that the guests enjoy and we are also introducing the Irish language to many Europeans including some unsuspecting English visitors. I must say I am beginning to enjoy having English guests as they are usually very friendly and easy to entertain. They are intrigued to find an Irishman out in the wilds of Africa and enjoy the story of how we ended up here. They are also partial to the Irish coffees that we are now serving regularly after dinner as they listen to a wide range of Irish tunes. I think it's called indoctrination or perhaps brainwashing!

I had a scare recently when my loyal little mongrel Bono almost croaked it. He lost his memory, his balance and it seemed like his whole central nervous system had broken down. I brought him to a local lady vet who was very helpful but not hopeful about his chances. She really wasn't sure what was wrong with him and gave me antibiotics more in hope than expectation. She mentioned possible snakebite, tick fever or distemper which seemed to me that she was covering every possibility. Bono was right off his food for six days and seemed to be on the way out. Until then he was a typical pound dog and he treated every meal like his last so it was distressing to see him like this. Anyway he started to respond slowly and bounced back to his young self. It seems he had a deep rooted ear infection that explained his loss of balance and the anti biotic did the trick. He has started running off with my shoes again so is clearly over the worst! Some friends from home have been asking me have I names for all the animals and pets that we are gathering around the lodge. I have to remind them that I am too busy for such sentimental nonsense and that this is a serious business I am trying to run. I want the staff to see that they have a responsible, mature, hard working boss who is focused on improving things around the farm and lodge. We continue to have our Monday morning meetings and everyone knows their role and working accordingly. The cooking has improved and we are now serving mostly fresh produce and sticking to country style cooking which the guests prefer. We have also changed the furniture around in the rooms and they now look less cluttered and more spacious. I sign off my February report back to all the family by mentioning that I will be home on February 27th for two weeks and suggest we meet up for an update. I am counting down the time as I have so much to tell after nearly eight week s here. There has been some low moments but mostly highs. I sign off with a P.S.-By the way Doris, Mabel, Louise, Harriot, Brigid, Margaret, Sally, Daisy and Bono say hello!!.

4

THE TIME TO REPAIR THE ROOF IS WHEN THE SUN IS SHINING!

Returning home at the end of February I was giddy with excitement. After two months away I couldn't wait to see the family and catch up with friends. In ways it had been the best and yet the most difficult two months of my life. I will never forget those first few weeks when I thought I was going slowly insane. I suppose it was part loneliness and also struggling to cope with the new surroundings and lifestyle. Also I couldn't help wondering was I mad to have taken such a financial risk and invested so much into this business. I believe now that part of the difficulty was having too much time alone and too much time to think. Long journeys cross country in an old unreliable uncomfortable car with no radio and stifling heat can play tricks with your mind. I definitely had moments of melancholy during this time when my head was full of bizarre and troubled thoughts. It was like solitary confinement in ways and the only redeeming feature was the beauty of the place and the surprises that lay around the next corner. It brought me into a deeper soul searching place that was uncomfortable at first and made sleep difficult and restless. I was happy to greet the mornings and hop out of bed early as it was better to be busy. Much later I was to appreciate this challenging time as it opened me up to a new level of personal awareness which I needed to explore.

I was so pleased to see everyone that it felt like I was back from space even though I was only two months away. Lots of people work abroad and leave their families for longer periods. I had met quite a few Germans particularly in Namibia who worked for German companies on three to six month engineering contracts and sometimes even longer. But for me it was the first time I had been away from the family for more than a few days. The main reason why I chose the end of February for a break was because of our youngest son Gareth's confirmation, an important event that should be shared by all the family. I met a few neighbours and friends and all were interested to hear how things were in Africa! The time flew and in no time I was heading back to the airport but in better spirits this time as my eldest son Anthony was coming with me for three months. He was in the middle of what you could describe as a gap year having finished secondary school the previous year and I thought it would be good experience for him at Ghaub. I also had plenty of work lined up for him.

March was an interesting time for us and again my monthly report captures the highlights and some further challenges. I began by sharing some tragic news. One of our staff Frieda who is twenty seven years old lost her daughter Beyozetha who was only three years of age. The little girl had been ill for some time and was taken to hospital suddenly after coming down with a temperature and fever. Frieda spent four nights with her in the hospital but then returned to work as the Doctors believed that Beyozetha was improving and would be fine. The next day we received a phone call at the lodge that the little mite had died during the night. Everyone was devastated and it was noticeable how the rest of the staff rallied around to support Frieda. It was obvious to me that she was encouraged to show her feelings and grieve openly. Then after many tears were shed she seemed to find acceptance quickly and started to plan for the wake and funeral. For me it was an example of the harshness of life in Africa. The infant mortality rate is high and life expectancy is still low despite improvements in health care and general hospital services. I dropped Frieda back to town and there was little conversation. The staff told me that there would be a service in four or five days as family and relations would need time to travel to the funeral from afar. I am told to expect some surprises as this won't be a traditional service as I know it. Nothing could have prepared me for what took place.

On the following Friday after we received word about the arrangements I set off again for Tsumeb sixty kilometres away with two of Frieda's friends to attend the service. We went first to her house to pay our respects and it was similar to a typical Irish wake. The family home was old but well maintained and part of a block of houses once owned by the mine workers from the now obsolete local copper mine. The houses were basic, solid structures with few frills. I was immediately taken with the formalities and the preparations being made for those expected to arrive as there was a large cooking pot hanging over an open fire just outside the front door of Frieda's house. We filed inside and the family were sitting around in mourning and prayer around the smallest white coffin I have ever seen. It was very emotional and Frieda seemed surprised but pleased to see us. We paid our respects and took a seat outside facing the house with about forty other people who had gathered. I got a few quizzical but not unfriendly looks as the only white person there. Dress was casual but the mood respectful. At ten minutes to 2.00pm a lady dressed in black arrived and I presumed she was there to lead the service. Then a couple of moments later I was tapped on the shoulder by a stranger and beckoned to follow him. Not sure what to expect I did as requested as my first thought was not to offend anyone by my presence. Out of the blue this guy asked would I mind driving the coffin to the cemetery as there were no other cars available. I hadn't noticed until then that there wasn't another vehicle at the house apart from our old Toyota Raider and naturally agreed to help in any way I could. I reversed the car up to the house and stood back as some of the males present placed the coffin in the back of the car which seemed to be the cue for others to pile in. It was quite a scene as we drove slowly through the streets of Tsumeb in our seriously overcrowded car with the occupants singing hymns in their own Damara language followed by the remaining mourners on foot. At the cemetery the ceremony followed much the same procedure as would happen at home except for the singing which I found very moving. Everyone present was invited to throw some clay onto the coffin in the open grave and there were a lot of tears. Overall it was a very spiritual occasion and there was a relaxed informality about it as there were some nervous giggles at one stage when everyone seemed to be waiting for someone else to decide what should happen next. A number of things struck me. There was no church service. The coffin had come directly from home to the cemetery. There was no priest or church celebrant and yet there seemed to be a clear ritual followed. After about an hour at the cemetery the mourners piled back into the car and we returned to Frieda's house. All present were invited to wash their hands together which is apparently a local custom and served a meal of pasta, grated carrot and chicken from the pot. I was overwhelmed by the occasion and I think my attendance at the funeral was unexpected but appreciated by Frieda and her family.

March brought many other special experiences and challenges. The weather began to change as the rainy season came to a conclusion. I am still reminded that a good day here is when the rain comes and not when the sun is shining brightly. Will I ever get used to that? I find it hard to imagine that there may come a time when I will pray for rain as the locals predict. Certainly at this stage I am enjoying the warm sunny days and the warm temperatures that greet you early most mornings. My mum used to say that March came in like a lamb and out like a lion. I think it was to an old Irish saying to remind you not to leave your winter vest off too soon! The seasons are very different here and although there are lambs and lions it's a March with a difference. My first priority on returning from home was to prepare for the tour operators arrival on the week-end of the 14th and 15th.I had left a long list of things to do in my absence and to be fair the staff had gone through everything in great detail. Andre had been busy as well and had arranged for an experienced caterer/chef to be present and to help the kitchen staff in their preparation and presentation of meals. I always thought we had two good chefs but really a little invention and imagination can make such a difference. Leonie, our marketing manager was also there and her influence and experience proved invaluable. She knew all the operators by name and her association with Guest Farm Ghaub seems to have convinced the operators that Ghaub is now heading in the right direction. We were all there to meet and greet the reps on arrival. Most were surprisingly young but there were a few who had been working in Namibian tourism for more than twenty years and more. There was a mix of gender and race and the atmosphere was friendly, relaxed and easy. We showcased the lodge generally and on the Saturday morning we brought everyone on a cave tour followed by a farm drive and a sun downer in the late afternoon. The Ghaub cave is a special feature on the property and actually has treasure status. Considered a national monument it is reported to be the third longest known cave in Namibia. As the largest cave called The Dragons breath is closed to the public we are mentioned in most guide books as a must see attraction. Ghaub cave has more than 2.5 kilometres of corridors and passageways and some brilliant examples of stalactites and stalagmites that are centuries old.

Sun downers are also an important feature as most of the leading lodges offer drives which typically take guests to a vantage point to watch the sun go down while having a cool drink and hopefully come across some animals on the way. We are lucky to have a few beautiful locations around the farm and the operators were very impressed with the scenery and views. Later on Saturday evening we have a Brai or Barbecue and stay up late chatting and telling jokes under the stars. The sky at night in the Southern hemisphere is so different and the planets and galaxies are clearly seen. We often turn out the lights totally to add to the effect and it is magical. On the Sunday after a late breakfast the operators begin to drift home as most have long journeys ahead of them. We ask for feedback and guidelines how we can improve the service and facilities at the lodge. The operators are brutally honest as they have the experience and know what guests are looking for. Mostly it's positive and any criticism is fair and helpful. We expect to have lots of new referrals from the companies as a result of this visit.

The change in ownership is receiving quite a bit of attention throughout the country and Guest Farm Ghaub receives some very complimentary reviews in the March edition of Travel News which is the most popular tourism magazine in Namibia. We are finally online and one can find out much more about the lodge at *ghaub@iway.na* We are also busy designing a new website at *www.ghaub.com* which we hope to have up and running soon. There is in fact a lot of interest in the Irish involvement at Ghaub which seems to have caught people's imagination. All of our visitors seem to be genuinely surprised and taken with the fact that it is possible for Europeans to get involved in a Namibian lodge. I received a phone call very early one morning recently from a Miss Ute from the afore mentioned Travel News and they want to visit us and do a large feature for their magazine for their May edition. Things are certainly beginning to look up. After the operators week-end we remained busy making small improvements around the lodge. We painted most of the buildings outside which improved the general appearance of the place. I have always emphasised to the staff how important first impressions are. When I arrived here first in January the lads used to make a pile of rubbish from the garden beside the front entrance and move it once a month when there was enough accumulated. I couldn't understand the thinking behind it and suggested they move it out of sight around the back of the house. They didn't seem to understand that this was the first thing the guests noticed when they arrived and it made a bad impression. There were a few other examples of old routines that needed to be changed and once it was explained to the staff they would sort it out straight away. I was beginning to get to know them all better now after three months and found them to be hard working, very willing and eager to please. I really had no complaints about their work ethic and figured out quickly who I could depend on and who I had to keep an eye on. We decided to make it a priority to improve the staff accommodation as it wasn't acceptable to have communal showers and bathrooms which the staff were sharing when we arrived. The staff have their own homes at what's called the Location just a

Kilometre from the main lodge. The houses are solid structures and well maintained. We set out to build a new bathroom and shower in each house and an extra room that could be used as another bedroom or sitting room or whatever the owner preferred. We had the job priced by a contractor in Grootfontein and he hopes to complete the work in six weeks. I was to discover that Namibian builders are like builders all over the world and that the promise of a fixed date for the completion of a job should be taken with a grain of salt!

I have also decided to open a shop at the lodge for the staff which Anthony will take charge of. It will mean that the staff will not have to travel to town for basic necessities and will never run out of essentials. Anthony is settling in well to his new surroundings and earning his keep. I am privately chuffed that he is working so hard and adapting to Namibian life. His knowledge of the computer has been a great help and we are now sending and receiving daily e-mails. We only have one line though which means that we can't receive phone calls when online. Anthony is up early each morning and busy helping outside with the guys in the garden mostly. He is learning to drive which should be a big help to us if he can share the driving responsibilities. There is plenty of room to learn as there is no traffic on the roads but yet you have to drive carefully as the surfaces can be slippery and there is always the danger of stray animals wandering out in front of you. Anthony has always been interested in animals and clearly enjoys the daily sightings of kudu, warthogs, duikers and baboons around the farm. The variety of exotic birds is plentiful too and there is a continuous chorus of music in the air. It is not unusual to have to chase the baboons off the garage roof first thing in the morning. They can be loud and aggressive when looking for food but usually run off when they hear humans approaching. We are still waiting for our first eggs and I am beginning to wonder was I taken in by the lady who sold me the chickens. Mind you they were only two Euros each. Anthony has started calling them Maryland, Drumstick, Thanksgiving and some other choice names which is a bit harsh! The farm remains busy and I make a point of seeing Billy, the farm manager, every other day. The maize is flourishing and now just ten weeks after planting it looks strong and healthy. Billy is hopeful of a good yield this year and reckons that we should be alright even if the rain stops completely soon. We sold a lot of cattle at the end of February and will be building up the herd later in the year with the emphasis on cows and calves. The grass is plentiful and it seems to this novice farmer that we could be cutting grass right now but the 'experts' say we have to wait! I am learning slowly about local rules and customs sometimes to my cost!

I got stopped in Grootfontein recently and was fined N$300 for not stopping at a stop sign. You wouldn't believe what happened. I was driving down a quiet street with little or no traffic in a small local town approaching a T junction. Looking both sides and seeing a clear road I slowed down but kept moving and suddenly a policeman jumped out from behind a sign and waved me down. Apparently I had broken a golden rule that a stop sign means stop even if the coast is clear. I was tempted to argue the point but as I wasn't quite sure how legal I really was at that time I thought better of it. It's amusing however as half the country seems to be driving around without insurance-especially the taxi drivers- and yet you can get fined for something as innocent as that. I swallow my pride, take my punishment and keep the ticket as a souvenir. I have noticed however that there is one local rule of the road that makes perfect sense and something we could introduce at home. When driving in town there is a law here that only allows you to park on the same side of the road that you are facing. Even if there is a space on the other side you must turn around and face in the same direction as when you come out of a space you are never crossing lanes. It works perfectly and should be introduced at home as our current system makes for hazardous driving through towns with narrow streets. The system here makes more sense.

I also had a surprise visit from Meath man Joe Mc Kenna who works for Coca Cola in Swaziland. He heard I was here from another friend Gerry Lynch who I played soccer with many years ago in Kentstown who also lives and works in Swaziland. Joe stayed two nights with two English friends he was travelling with and we had a great chat and discovered that we had many mutual acquaintances in County Meath. It was a great fillip to have such unexpected company. We also had a visit from a young couple who are working as overseas volunteers in a school in Northern Namibia. The young girl was English from London and she enjoyed her stay so much that she promised to return soon with some of her volunteer friends. This was to become a regular feature and we now have had lots of overseas volunteers come to stay at the lodge as the word has spread. We always try to give them a favourable rate and many have been back whenever they get some time off from their demanding jobs.

We started playing soccer every Sunday in January and have kept it up whenever the lodge is quiet at week-ends. The staff are all enthusiastic and even the girls join in with enthusiasm. I received a present of a full set of football jerseys from my friend Christy Hand from Kilcormac when I was last home and we now get a chance to show them off after a challenge from the neighbouring farm workers at Toggenburg. We had played them earlier at our place when the game had to be blown up early before a riot ensued. They play in a local soccer league and are well organised if a little aggressive in my opinion. Well this time we were ready and got our retaliation in first! They had one white person who is the farmer's son but otherwise like us the team consisted of the farm and lodge workers. I have to confess that I got a bit carried away and had to substitute myself at half time for safety reasons. Either I would have a heart attack or start a row and I was surprised at how competitive I became. Anthony replaced me and we held out for a deserved 1–1 draw and honour was restored. The team and our supporters sang the all the way home in our seriously overcrowded Land Cruiser. Just another memorable day in a long list of experiences that I will never forget.

On Easter Sunday I brought Anthony to the service at the Maria Bronn School. By now we were warmly greeted each week and on this occasion it was particularly special. I was tempted to put a sign on my door 'he is gone -he is risen' when Anthony came looking for me! At first I was disappointed to discover that all the children had gone home for the holiday and there were just the nuns and a few locals present. But the sisters sang their hearts out and then danced up the aisle at the offertory. It was like something out of Sister Act and Whoopi Goldberg would have felt at home! I am convinced that RTE should come out to broadcast this unbelievable event and promise myself to contact the head of Religious affairs at RTE soon. I honestly believe it would bring people back to the church and I intend to keep coming every week if at all possible. I forgot to mention St Patrick's Day which we celebrated in our own special way. I brought some green, white and orange balloons and displayed the Irish flag at several central points around the lodge. The staff were fascinated to hear the story of how St Patrick drove the snakes out of Ireland. They are all terrified of snakes and I think their appreciation of all things Irish has increased as a result. The guests also joined in celebrating our national feast day and appreciated the complimentary Irish coffees. The month turns out to be an enjoyable one overall and with Anthony for company I am beginning to feel more at home here. I am aware that I am changing to some extent and starting to appreciate this opportunity more and more. It feels like a privilege to be here and my energy levels and tolerance are growing. It is inspirational and there are times when I definitely feel as content as I have ever been. I could happily settle here if the family could be here with me. Who knows what lies ahead but just maybe it could be possible? I have actually experienced moments of extreme clarity of thought and inspiration recently. I can only describe it as a feeling of accessing a part of me that I have never been aware of before. My thinking is clearer and anything seems possible. It's a positive but more than that as I feel more creative than ever before and have loads of ideas about projects, stories, jokes and observations that never crossed my mind before. I was to continue having these moments of clarity over the following months inspired by my surroundings and my experiences in this beautiful place.

When in Rome

I was at this stage well adapted to life in Namibia and beginning to think and feel like a local. When I travelled to town I was no longer treated like a tourist and received nods and waves of recognition from new friends and acquaintances. I still held onto that sense of wonder and awe that I experienced on my first visit the previous year. But now it was the people that made the biggest impression on me and challenged something within me about my own lack of selflessness and generosity of spirit. Let me introduce you to just some of the characters I met and became friendly with.

Mika, our lodge manager, continued to amaze me with his dedication, his willingness and his attitude towards his work and his interactions with the other staff and guests. He really is a treasure and our most important asset at the lodge. I can trust him implicitly and he is so conscientious and honest that I don't have to worry whenever I have to be away from the lodge. His manner with the guests is exemplary and he is always thoughtful and welcoming as they arrive. Their first impressions are always positive as a result and the guests often comment to me about how lucky we are to have him. Mika has a great attitude with the staff as well and there is obviously a mutual respect between them. It is not easy sometimes for local people in positions of authority giving orders to their peers and getting the best out of them. I am aware in other situations this breaks down through jealousy and petty squabbling. Mika is able to remain friendly with the staff while keeping his distance as he is responsible for delegating jobs and making sure they are carried out properly. I depend on him so much that now we have a good working relationship and I am aware that this makes other people uncomfortable. There is an unwritten, unspoken arrangement here that maintains a distance between white and black even when there is mutual respect. I have been struggling with the occasional racist comments that I hear in certain company. This is new territory for me and colour has never been an issue but you can't avoid it here as Namibia like all African Countries struggles to treat people equally for obvious historical and

61

political reasons. I can only honour my own beliefs regarding what I believe to be right and have learned to choose my words at times. I have been advised more than once not to trust the black people. 'They will rob and cheat you if they get the chance so you must never let your guard down and keep your distance and your boundaries very clearly defined.'- I really react to this type of generalization and this notion that you must treat everyone with an element of distrust. I do try to understand where these prejudices come from and engage in frank discussion with some people that I know I can share my real feelings with. But there are some who are unwilling to even consider that their stance is perhaps extreme and borne out of fear that to change it would somehow weaken their position. I have to respect that I am still new here and a visitor to their country and strive to reach a balance that allows me to honour my own beliefs and still respect the views of others. But I will always treat people as I find them and will trust anyone unless they give me reason not to. Mika has never given me reason to question his dedication to the lodge and I appreciate how crucial he is to this whole operation.

Most of the staff are just as committed as Mika. Immanuel who is a Kavango from the North East of the Country is another incredibly loyal and hardworking member of the team. His duties include responsibility for the upkeep of the garden and the surrounds. He is a driver also and general maintenance manager and really a very skilled jack of all trades. His English is not great but he works with a smile and he seems to always know what's needed to be done as regularly when I go looking for him to sort something out he is usually already two steps ahead of me. He has a great attitude and Kavango people seem to me to be hard working, conscientious and family conscious as well. Immanuel or Tato as we call him for short is always sending money home to his family and looking after his relations. He could earn a fortune in Ireland with his skills but realistically he will probably never own a passport and has no ambition to move away from his family. The different tribal backgrounds are very interesting and I am slowly also beginning to appreciate the subtle differences between the Ovambo people, the Kavangos and the Damara as we have quite a mix of workers from the different tribes. There are some lodges that refuse to employ different groups as they believe that they are unable to work closely together without their cultural differences creating problems. Other lodges only employ men as they wish to avoid staff relationships developing and tension emerging as a result. We don't seem to have those problems so far as we also have Damara, Kavango, Ovambo and Herero staff among the group. They all certainly have their own distinctive traditions and beliefs which are not always clear to me. They also have their own languages which are fascinating to listen to and very musical. Damara is particularly interesting as it is one of those African languages with clicks and strange sounds and impossible for Europeans to imitate. But English is widely spoken by most people and as such communication is easy. Afrikaans is still the language of choice but more and more English is spoken which makes it easy for tourists and visitors from Europe who all seem to have passable English.

I have also made friends in Grootfontein and Tsumeb which are the local towns I usually visit. Both are about fifty Kilometres away from the lodge in opposite direction and every journey to town brings some surprises. I often meet Lucas at the garage in Tsumeb when I call to fill up! Lucas is a brother or Martin who works with us at the lodge and you can see the family resemblance. He tells me that he works 12 hour shifts with no break seven days a week. He earns about N\$1,400 per month which is roughly 120 Euro which I find incredible. This seems like a clear breach of local labour law rules that insists that employees should only work six days a week and never more than 7.5 hour shifts. Clearly there is such demand for work that conditions can be extremely harsh as jobs will be quickly taken by others if a person questions their conditions of employment. I have also been made aware that there is no social welfare here or the dole as we know it. If you are not working then there is no assistance which makes you wonder how people manage. Lucas remains upbeat and looks forward to payday at the end of each month and is planning to get married next year. I usually give him a few dollars extra to supplement his income as he is always helpful and serves with a smile. I also met a guy called Cornelius at the Bank in Grootfontein and he has also become a good friend. He has worked his way up to a position of manager and from day one he has made things easier for me whenever I have had banking problems. He is smart and personable and has been out to see the lodge. He is clearly an example of someone who worked his way through the system through hard work and also having a good manner and attitude. He hopes to receive a more senior managerial role within the Bank in the coming years and is ambitious to go as far as he can. He deserves to succeed as he has a warm personality that comes easy to him. Meeting different local people certainly added to my experience and enhanced my appreciation of your average Namibian. I was finding my feet and fitting in and beginning to rearrange my priorities.

Moving into April I was conscious that if I was at home this would mean the U.S. Masters from Augusta, the Grand National from Aintree and the start of the football championship in County Meath! This year was very different as I forgot the Masters was on and still don't know who won the National. Here it has been a month of early morning starts, feeding animals, painting outhouses, waiting on tables and a host of other jobs. April started as it does all over the world. April Fools is apparently a worldwide phenomenon as the staff at the lodge played tricks on each other. One of the lads arrived in to work an hour early as he was told I wanted to see him as he was in trouble! April fool. One of the girls received a live turtle in a parcel from overseas and as she is terrified of anything with more than two legs she didn't appreciate the surprise! I had to be careful all day but it was all good innocent fun. We also started a major clean up operation around the garden of the lodge and took down around twenty large dead trees which were becoming dangerous and unsightly. It was heavy work with tractors, chainsaws, ropes and a wing and a prayer. We were lucky that nobody was injured or that we didn't take out some good healthy trees as cries of TIMBER rang out around the garden as these huge old trees crashed down around us. For two full days with the help of four guys from the farm we cleared out the dead wood and the place looked so much better. Andre arrived mid morning from Okahandja by plane with a co pilot friend. He flew in a small 4 seater plane over the house and landed on the road causing great excitement. I went down in the buggy to pick them up when I met them coming back up the road towards me and had to pull over to let them pass. They parked the plane outside the front gate, stayed a few hours and took off again late afternoon. It was like something out of Biggles or Wilbur Smith.

Then it was time to cut the hay finally as the rains seemed to be finished for the season. There was a hive of activity for a full week around the lodge and neighbouring fields as the grass was cut and bailed with an old Welger machine that looked like an antique from another time. But it was functional and although slow by Irish standards it got the job done. Bales were gathered up as you would do at home and brought by trailer to the farm and stacked away for feeding later in the season when the grass gets scarce. Hard to believe that we could have six months now without a drop of rain. The landscape is changing and already beginning to look brown and dry. The maize could have done with one more last good fall of rain which was expected but didn't arrive. As a result the harvest may not be as good as first forecasted which is disappointing. Surprisingly we have had some very cold nights recently with temperatures close to freezing which can also have disastrous consequences for the maize but so far we seem to be alright. Some farms in the South have apparently lost their whole season due to unseasonable early frost.

On April 7th we reached a milestone and a target that we had set ourselves in January. We had a full house at the lodge for the first time this year. We actually had twenty five guests staying as we had a booking for four South African families who were travelling in convoy on the way to Zambia. We had to put some mattresses out on the floors for children as we ran out of beds but it was a good problem to have and it boosted our income for the month significantly. We have continued going to the Maria

Bronn School each Sunday and each week the experience is up-lifting. I decided to donate a new P.A. system for the church having spoken to the head, Sister Lidwina. I really wanted to give something back as I felt privileged to be there each week. It cost about the same amount as two tickets for the Prince concert in Croke Park in July in Dublin that I nearly bought last time I was home but decided against as I couldn't justify the price. I told Sister Lidwina to think of it as a present from Ireland and asked her not to make a fuss about it. The following Sunday having had the system fitted by a friend from Grootfontein they had the first ever service with sound at the Maria Bronn school. At the end of the mass Sister Lidwina came out to the altar to address the gathering which consisted of about 300 children, 30 nuns, around 10 locals and one very white looking Irish man! She began by saying how happy she was to finally have sound in the church after all these years and she wanted to thank Mr Gerry from Ireland for his gift and invited the children to sing a song of gratitude. Well I didn't know where to look and afterwards all the nuns and every single child had to shake hands with the kind Irishman and an orderly queue formed! It was almost like a papal audience and I felt very humbled, just a bit embarrassed and moved by the experience.

The following day we had another drama when one of the children at the location (the staff quarters) scalded herself with boiling water and I had to rush her to hospital in Tsumeb. She received serious third degree burns to her leg but has since recovered remarkably well. Every month since I arrived here I have had at least one trip to the hospital with a sick or injured child. I have to say that the medical service would put us to shame. Despite poor facilities and a lack of qualified personnel the level of care is remarkable and efficient. There are no queues in casualty and patients are seen quickly. On this occasion we wait ten minutes to be seen and the visit including dressings cost N$20 or two Euro.

Around the middle of the month we had a lady V.I.P. visitor from South Africa called Ron Swilling. She is a free lance journalist who was asked by Travel News to visit Ghaub in order to write a feature for their July edition. Well we rolled out the red carpet and tried to showcase the lodge at its best. Ms Swilling only stayed 24 hours and seemed impressed although she gave very little away. We are hopeful that a favourable review will bring in bookings and we will get an immediate response. I enclose a brief summary of her article which appeared in a subsequent edition which we were more than pleased with and it was to prove to be a huge help in spreading the news of Guest Farm Ghaub to a wider audience.

"Driving the gravel road into Ghaub, the verdant hills transform into rows of healthy green maize, and then into a sprawling, clean shaven lawn dotted with palm trees and old style mission houses, rolling into wild bush and the Otavi mountains. A feeling not just of history, but of tranquillity pervades Guest Farm Ghaub. It's more than the old fashioned style of the buildings; a deeply felt peace has permeated into the land and air at Ghaub. The establishment, situated on the 11,800 hectare Ghaub farm, was formerly a Lutheran mission station established in 1895 and operating until 1968. A few of the original buildings remain, while two extra blocks of room were added retaining the same style of wide verandas and high ceilings and increasing the number of spacious rooms to ten."

The next piece is particularly interesting and raised the awareness of the Irish connection for many of our visitors.

"Irish-born, part owner, Gerry Cooney came for a Namibian holiday in August 2007, staying at Guest Farm Ghaub for two nights. He so enjoyed the atmosphere of the place, that on leaving he commented "I could stay here forever." The outcome was that he definitely could, as the farm was up for sale. Gerry's life changed dramatically when he bought the farm with Andre Compion three months later. He says that the place found him.

Another Ghaub gentleman is Mika Shapwanale, manager of the guest farm. Mika born in Ovambo land in northern Namibia, has worked here for ten years, beginning in the gardens, learning English, Afrikaans and German, and progressing to restaurant manager, barman and waiter, improving his English continually by conversing with the guests. He began to take farm and cave tours, and became active manager at the beginning of 2006.

We join Mika in the trusty old Land Cruiser for one of the farm drives offered at Ghaub, ending in the hills for sundowners. Passing through farm gates, we stop to look at a few Bushman rock engravings, stepping on fresh aardvark tracks, and visit an old cemetery with graves of missionaries and German soldiers. Grey lauries fly through the trees and warthog families run across the road. Mika identifies the different trees, pointing out a large Marula tree, it's fruit collected in the month of May to make Marula juice and jam, served at breakfast on the Ghaub tables with delicious homemade bread. (review of Ghaub by Travel News Sept 2008).

It was around this time that I decided to enquire locally about life insurance as I was unable to arrange it at home. Apparently if you are working outside Ireland you do not qualify for life cover. I called into the local branch of Bank Windhoek in Grootfontein, where my friend Cornelius works, and was introduced to a straight talking ex rugby playing former police officer Afrikaner. He talked me through the policy and referred me to a local Doctor for a necessary medical before the contract could be signed. He was helpful if a bit clipped which I found many of the Africans/Namibian/German people to be. Sometimes there is a lack of warmth in the greeting and very UN Irish like! I think I became a bit of a curiosity as I greeted everyone the same which some people seemed uncomfortable with. My visit to the Doctor was one of those occasions! Initially our exchanges were formal and matter of fact but subsequently we hit it off well and the Doctor was to become a regular visitor to the lodge with her family. With all the tests done I was hoping to be soon worth more dead than alive!

We have also been busy this month working on the staff houses at their location. We arranged for a building firm to fit bathrooms and toilets in each of the four houses belonging to the staff as mentioned previously. The work has been slow as the foreman is rarely there and apparently busy looking after other sites despite our arrangement and agreement that he would be a constant presence. I have had to remind him that we want the job completed satisfactorily in eight weeks before full payment would be made. This was to prove another challenge for me in dealing with business people and I learned quickly that builders are the same the world over. "I'll be back tomorrow to finish that job." Never believe it! The staff though are delighted with their extensions and morale is even better as a result. I discovered that the girls particularly were pleased that they would no longer have to go out in the dark late at night to use the bathroom as they are terrified of the possibility of coming across snakes and other animals. I have noticed too that they all cut the grass around their houses regularly for much the same reason to discourage uninvited visitors.

We had an unexpected visitor recently too that also contributed to my growing list of what I call my must learn quicker list! A white van with the name Cenored in bold print on it's side drove in and the driver passed by the office without stopping or introducing himself. I was developing an issue with visitors driving onto the property without first calling in to explain the reason for their visit. It's just a matter of courtesy for me and a matter of security. Mika explained that Cenored was the local Electricity supply board or the equivalent of the E.S.B. and any time they visit it usually means trouble! Well the problem soon became clear as the driver announced that he was here to disconnect us for failing to pay our electricity bill on time. Well as you can imagine I wasn't having that and insisted that there was no way I was going to allow him to cut us off as we had guests to consider(which was true) and besides we were planning to pay the bill the next day when shopping in town(which wasn't)! Anyway to make a long story even longer the guy said he would give us 24 hours to pay or else he would be back. I had been planning to go to Tsumeb next day and so having weighed up the options decided that I would have to keep my promise in this instance at least. Next day I reluctantly visited Cenored and met with the manager who was younger than I expected and quite unfriendly. He explained in front of a packed waiting room that I would have to pay a reconnection fee with the full bill. Well I again put my foot down as we hadn't been disconnected so how could there be a reconnection fee. Besides I was here to pay the bill in full and suggested that he was trying to hoodwink me. We had a right old argument in front of a curious audience in an overcrowded office with several witnesses, none of whom seemed to be taking my side! I was really chancing my arm and luckily he relented first and accepted my initial offer. But he invited me to join him in his office when I had settled the bill and for a moment I thought I had taken things too far. As our exchange had been hot and heavy I didn't know what to expect. Turns out he apologised for his attitude which was unnecessary as I felt at least half responsible. He then asked me could I sell him some meat from the farm! You couldn't make it up. He was willing to pay good money for Kudu meat or beef. I said we could do business and promised to call. The list was growing!

We had a visit too from my sister's Evelyn's husband Ian recently too which Anthony and I enjoyed and we caught up on all the news from home. He was working in South Africa for a few days having travelled over with horses for the Curragh Bloodstock and flew up to Windhoek before hiring a car to come to the lodge. We went to meet him in Otavi and he stayed for three nights B and B (Beer and Biltong as we called it!).Biltong is dried meat which is a popular snack here and Ian particularly enjoys it. We went for a long drive around the land and came across lots of animals and had a nice sun downer at one of the highest points on the farm. We planned introducing horse trails and overnight camping for guests and Ian would bring his experience with horses to help us out. He hopes to come back with Evelyn in July and by then we will definitely be offering horse riding to guests.

Anthony continues to work hard and has adapted well to African lifestyle. His friends wouldn't believe that he is often in bed before 10.00pm. He especially enjoys the work with the animals and meeting guests. The chickens are finally laying eggs and although it has taken two months I get a great kick out of collecting the eggs in the morning. You can clearly taste the difference between our own free range eggs and the ones you buy in the supermarket.

We also had a week-end in Swakopmund recently for a bit of a break and to do a bit of marketing of the lodge. Swakopmund is a five hour drive towards the coast but on good surface roads and across interesting landscapes. You really begin to appreciate the vastness of Namibia on long drives like this as the scenery is breathtaking at times across miles of barren desert. You notice different things when driving in the opposite direction that we travelled as a family on that first fateful day. As you get closer to the coast the surroundings change dramatically and suddenly the sea appears in the distance which is always a welcoming sight after such a long journey. We stay with Leonie and her family, our marketing manager, in Walvis Bay and enjoy their hospitality. The feedback from the Operators week-end has been very positive according to Leonie and advanced bookings are strong. Otherwise it's business as usual and never a dull moment. Every day brings surprises and you learn something new. I recently learned that you should never underestimate a squirrel! You might think you can outsmart them but you never will. They can squeeze into the tiniest gap and I believe it's impossible to ever build a squirrel proof building or structure. Despite my best efforts they continue to break into the chicken house but only seem interested in the meal and seeds. I am convinced they carry around miniature drills and tools hidden on their person! They are too smart for me anyway. Also I have learned that baboons can't count past three. If four people go into a field and only three come out they are unable to work out that someone has stayed behind apparently. So don't forget that as it might come in useful someday! Overall April was a busy but productive month. We are often working sixteen hour days seven days a week but I am happy to put the time in. I still miss home hugely and there are some dark moments when you feel unappreciated and forgotten about. If anyone at home thinks I am on a junket sitting out under the sun and sipping cocktails they are greatly mistaken. This is the hardest thing I have ever done but there are many rewards. I particularly enjoyed Ian's visit this month as he was obviously reminded of his early years growing up in Rhodesia long ago before he decided to come to Ireland. I was intrigued at his appreciation of plants and local shrubs which he had forgotten about and now they reminded him of another time. It gave us time to chat in a way that we have never done before and at one stage I thought he was seriously considering staying with us. What would I say to my sister Evelyn?

5

THE DARKEST HOUR IS THE ONE
BEFORE THE DAWN!

Although I experienced amazing moments of serenity and peacefulness in Africa I also had some challenging times that tested my patience and fortitude. I had to learn quickly that not everyone is full of the milk of human kindness! There is always somebody looking to take advantage and you have to have your wits about you working in the service industry. I was winging it for ages and making it up as I went along. This was such a new experience for me that I really had to stretch myself to survive. I had only ever worked in the caring profession although I am not sure what that means. I suppose I fell into different jobs over the years rather than it been part of a grand master plan. When I think back now there was certainly a lot of chance involved in my choice of career. I had started as a Child Care worker spending time in children's homes before moving on to the area of special needs with the St Michael's House organization. Then on to Finglas Children's Centre for nine years in Juvenile Detention before moving on to Addiction treatment and Counselling. Each position I enjoyed for a time but the work was always demanding and stressful. I never imagined I would work till retirement age at sixty five in the same field and somehow knew I would end up doing something very different which would be outdoors and possibly involving animals. I suppose when this opportunity came along I was ready and half expected it.

I find now that guests are always interested in how I ended up in Namibia. Almost everyone asks what did I do before I bought the business here. This conversation often begins as I serve drinks in the evening time after waiting on tables over dinner. 'Actually I was a Counsellor in an Addiction centre at home in

Dublin', I usually reply as I top up the drinks feeling very aware of the incongruity of what I am saying! How much farming experience did you have is usually the next question? Absolutely none I reply and yes it's true the farm is nearly 30,000 acres in total! Have I mentioned that before? The conversation usually develops from there and I must say that the typical reaction is amazement although I do get the occasional person questioning my sanity!

If I have learned one thing since this whole venture began it is the importance of surrounding yourself with the right people in business and involving those you can trust and depend on. I am lucky to have good people with me who keep my feet on the ground. I am not foolish or easily taken in but you certainly do have to keep your wits about you here. I have a few personal rules and guidelines and one is if something looks too good to be true it probably is! There are lots of people who are only too happy to relieve any unsuspecting innocent of their hard earned money given the opportunity. I became aware of this phenomenon very soon after arriving here as I began to receive offers of incredible wealth in exchange for my Bank details on a weekly basis. You wouldn't believe how persistent some of these scammers are but some are extremely clever and do manage to relieve the gullible and naive of serious amounts of money. I understand that several lodges in Namibia have been caught out with a very clever scam that again fits into the too good to be true category. A typical rouse would begin with an innocent enquiry about availability at the lodge via the internet. When the request is for more than three rooms and for more than three of four nights you become immediately suspicious. Typically the bogus enquiry will request four or more rooms for six or more nights and ask for the total cost which they offer to pay in advance. You would imagine this seems innocent enough and sounds like a good booking which will raise occupancy levels. If the total bill amounts to N$6,000 for example the enquirer will offer to pay by credit card in advance and again it seems like a good deal and you can decide to confirm or waitlist the booking. So far so good. However what really happens is that the bogus operator cancels the payment unknown to the vendor before cancelling the booking four weeks or so before the guests are due to arrive and then requests their money back which they are entitled to do. The lodge manager may see nothing wrong with this but the person using an untraceable number or e-mail address receives the full amount for a substantial booking that was never paid for in the first place. Believe it or not but this scam has caught out many lodges although few would care to admit it. The only way to guard against this particular rouse is to insist that the booking is secured but credit card details will only be used to confirm the booking and no monies will be charged until the arrival of the guests. Usually that will be the last you will hear from the enquirer and you put it down to experience and thank your lucky stars that you have followed the recommended course of action. You have to be careful though as sometimes a quite legitimate booking may appear like a scam and you have to respond appropriately or risk missing out on some welcome business.

The other type of scam letters are easier to detect. The ones that promise you a small fortune in exchange for your Bank details are priceless and sometimes very funny as they are so obvious. Typically these will be written in pigeon English full of grammatical mistakes and smelling of desperation. Hard to believe that they actually ever succeed but I suppose that the perpetrators work off the chance of something like 1% of respondents been seduced by the promise of riches for little in return. No matter how many times you receive these unbelievable offers knowing full sure that they should be binned immediately perhaps some people can't help thinking that just maybe once you could hit the jackpot ! I have to admit that occasionally I have allowed myself to briefly go down that road despite myself. I include just a few examples of e-mails I received within one month alone. See can you spot the anomalies and ask yourself honestly would you have been tempted!

Example 1

From "Peter Mc Wealth"<petermcwealth1551@msn.com>

To <undisclosed-recipients:>

Subject World Fund Discovery Management and payment Bureau.

From: Dr Peter Mc Wealth

Director: World Fund Discovery

Tel: 00447892832587

This letter is from World Fund Discovery Management and Payment Bureau newly established by the World Financial Service Authority United States of America /United Kingdom. This body was set up to discover an outstanding unpaid fund being owed to Government or Individuals all over the world through contract payment, inheritance and lottery winning prize awards. It will interest you to know that we have discovered an outstanding unpaid/unclaimed sum of money in favour of your name and a mandate has been given to this body World Fund Discovery Management and Payment Bureau to ensure that this fund gets to you without delay. Note that a special payment arrangement has been made to deliver this fund to you through diplomatic means of payment or alternatively come in person to any of our payment offices in Europe, America or Asia. You are advised to furnish this office with your contact information to enable us to open up communication with you regarding the release of your fund immediately.

Thanks.

Yours Truly.

Dr Peter Mc Wealth (Director)

I suppose the name is a bit of a giveaway! The next request would inevitably be for your Bank details once communication is established. Some others are less obvious.

Example 2

To Guest Farm Ghaub

From "James Ponder" <jj.ponder1@yahoo.com>

Subject-Your Kindly gesture is Needed . . .

Dear Sir,
Thank you for the bookings and confirmations. The total cost of the accommodation is quite okay by me and I am ready to pay the bills. Also I want you to help me send another N$6,000 to a travel agent who has issued my guests air flight tickets to your hotel. The N$6,000 that will be sent to the agent is for the ticket fare for my guests which will be deducted from my credit card. Also I am compensating you with the sum of N$500 for the transfer fee and for your efforts. Please note that I should have given the travel agency my credit card details for him to deduct the ticket funds but he told me he doesn't have the facilities to charge or debit credit cards., so that's why I bring my vote of confidence in you and I don't want you to betray that vote of confidence I put in you so I want you to transfer the funds to him after you have make the charges after the money charged from my credit card has entered your account you can make the transfer to the agent. So the charges you make on my credit card will be.
Accommodation fee n$17,595.00
Agent fee for shipping N$6,000
Transfer fee to the agent in West Africa due your efforts (n$500). Note that my credit card will be charged for the amounts above. Please do get back to me if you are in the office right now so that I can forward my credit card details to you, then you can charge full amount and transfer the agent funds to him. I await your response.
James.

I must say I love the line "I bring my vote of confidence in you and I don't want you to betray it"! This is a familiar expression now and straight away places a serious question regarding the validity of the request.

Example 3

From "FNB"<risk@fnb.co.za>

To <undisclosed-recipients:>

Subject Online account violation

Dear Sir,

Due to concerns for the safety of your FNB account we have issued this warning message severally but some FNB customers fail to heed this warning. It has come to our attention that FNB account holders are subject to most phishing attacks hence your FNB account information needs to be verified as part of our continuing commitment and ceaseless efforts to protect your account in this year 2009 and to reduce the instance of fraud on our website.

If you could please take 5–30 minutes from your online experience to verify your access on our SSL. Your FNB account service will not be interrupted and will continue as normal with full protection. Protect your account with the FNB link provided below.https://www.fnb.co.za/securitycentre/login.html

Bank and stay safe online,

Security management,

First National Bank.

This is a tricky one as it appears to be correspondence from ones established Bank but seemingly when you attempt to verify your details your information is intercepted and you risk significant losses from your account which only comes to light on receipt of your following statement.

Example 4

From Mrs Susan Shabangu < Mrs Susanshabangu 1955@gmail.com>

To <undisclosed-recipients;>

Subject Re Susan Shabangu

From Mrs Susan Shabangu,

Deputy Minister of Safety and Security,

South Africa.

e-mail;mrs susan shabangu 1955@gmail.com

(please contact my son Mr Terry Shabangu.

Dear Sir/Madam,
First let me introduce myself as Mrs Susan Shabangu, a mother of 3 children and the DEPUTY Minister of SAFETY AND SECURITY SINCE 29th April 1966 to date under the auspices of the President of South Africa Mr Thabo Mbeki. After due deliberation with my children I decided to contact you for your assistance in standing as a beneficiary to the sum of US14.5m(fourteen Million, five hundred dollars only).

You can view my profile at my website www.gov.za then click on Deputy Minister and click on safety and security finally, click on my name then Susan Shibangu.

The proposal after the swearing in ceremony making me Deputy Minister of safety and security, my husband Mr Ndelebe Shabangu died while he was on an official trip to Trinidad and Tobago in 1996.After his death I discovered that he had funds in a dollar account which amounted to the sum of US 14.5M with a security and finance institution in South Africa of which I will divulge information to you when I get your full consent and support to go for a change of beneficiary and subsequent transfer of the funds into a comfortable and conducive account of your choice. This fund emanated as a result of an over-invoiced contract which he executed with the government of South Africa. Though I assisted him in getting this contract I never knew it was over-invoiced by him. I am afraid that the government of South Africa might start to investigate on contracts awarded from 1990 to date. If they discover this money in his Bank account they will confiscate it and seize his assets here in South Africa and this will affect my political career in government .I want your assistance in opening an account with bankers through my banker so that this fund could be wired into your account directly without any hitch. As soon as the fund gets to your account you are expected to move it immediately into another personal bank account in your country. I will see to it that the account is not traced from South Africa. As soon as you have confirmed the fund into your account I will send my eldest son with my attorney to come to your country to discuss on business investments. For your assistance I am offering you 20% .However you have to assure me and also be ready to go into agreement with me that you will not elope with my fund. If you agree to my terms kindly as a matter of urgency send me an email. Due to my sensitive position in the South African Government please do not call on the office line because of the sensitivity of this transaction except to the above direct line.

Regards,
Susan Shibangu.

Unbelievable really but yet the amount of time and thought it takes to come up with something like this and to address it to a complete stranger. Can you imagine a Deputy Minister taking such an action in your country. Perhaps you can!

Example 5

This particular one was from a gentleman who proved to be extremely persistent before he finally accepted that he was trying to fool the wrong people. There were several exchanges of correspondence before he tired of it and moved on the next unsuspecting victim. The following is just a short sample of the E -mails we received from him over a two week period. I suppose it could have been a she!

From Edmund Brooks <edmundbrooks04@yahoo.co.uk

To Guest Farm Ghaub

Subject Booking total cost

I got your e-mail and I appreciate your kind response. The group shall be staying for 10 days that will commence on the 10th to 20th of November. Request 3 Double rooms for 10 nights and payment will be made in full by credit card immediately. Please get back to me with the grand total for the time requested.
Your prompt response will be appreciated.
Thanks for your co-operation,
Dr Edmund Brooks.
Tel-00447031921122.
I replied with the following letter.

Dear Sir,
Thank you once again for your enquiry and for your interest in Guest Farm Ghaub. As previously explained we do have availability on the nights you request and I can confirm that we have provisionally reserved three double rooms for your guests. We look forward to welcoming them to Ghaub and I am sure they will enjoy the facilities we have to offer and the peaceful atmosphere which exists here. Please check out our new website at www. ghaub.com or more information.

Again I inform you that we only require your credit card details to secure the booking and the information will be retained for guarantee purposes. Full payment can be made on arrival or on completion of your stay.

Regards,

Gerry Cooney.

There was a further exchange of mail when Dr Brooks did his best to pay his bill in advance but eventually he relented. There were a number of familiar warning signals about this particular booking. Nobody ever wishes to stay for ten nights at the same lodge in Namibia when on holiday. Unless they are working or staying for a long period of time there it is unheard of for visitors to stay more that two or three nights in reality. We have had the odd exception but very rarely. We had a lovely German couple stay two weeks with us and used the lodge as a base to travel to local places of interest including Etosha at least twice but they were the exception. Namibia is so vast and there is so much to see that the challenge is to reach a balance between seeing the sights but not spend too much time in the car. But typically it's one or two nights here and there before moving on to the next treat.

This was just a small selection of many bogus enquiries we received within a particular month and just a flavour of what most lodges have to deal with. The guests who do arrive are generally trustworthy and pay their bills in full without complaint. We have never had a problem with credit card fraud or a bad debt. Guests typically leave their rooms as they find them and do not tend to bring souvenirs with them from the lodge. In the service industry however you must keep your wits about you at all times as there is always someone out there who will chance their luck if they think they can get away with it. These are not typically disadvantaged desperate people who are struggling to survive but clever opportunists who prey on the unsuspecting.

6

ONLY LOOK BACK IF YOU WANT TO GO IN THAT DIRECTION!

During the month of May I tried to get to grips with the demands of the business. After all this was not just a lifestyle change but an opportunity to build a future for Marian and the boys. I am the first to admit that I am not the most organised when it comes to financial matters. I have never worried about money or ever had any huge ambitions to amass a fortune. Once I had enough to get by and the family were looked after I was always relatively happy. I am sure I lost opportunities along the way to get rich quickly but perhaps declining offers was the wiser course of action in hindsight. I never had much but I never owed anyone anything and that was the principle I operated under. This was different as I had staked more than I could afford into this property and would be paying back for a long time if the business went belly up. No job I ever had compensated me for the work I did and I suppose if I was motivated by money I would have made a career change many years ago. So I faced into the challenge of running a lodge and keeping an eye on a large farm with enthusiasm, vigour and a wing and a prayer! The staff were making my position easier as there was a mutual respect from day one and a relaxed but yet busy energy always. I had very few problems during my first four months but now had a good idea who I could depend on and who I had to keep half an eye on. Then suddenly I had to deal with my first real personnel problem and was aware that this would be a test case for others who were waiting to see how I would respond to my youngest member of staff. Erenst was 21 years old and his mother was one of my chefs which complicated matters. Like any good Irish Mother Martha always stood up for Erenst and excused his erratic application to his work by blaming everyone else except himself. Some days it was Mika that was the problem. Now Mika is the most inoffensive reasonable man you could ever meet and that was never going to wash with me. She also told me stories of how Erenst missed his father who had left home when he was young and how he desperately wanted to better himself to make her proud. This may well have been all true but Erenst was still pushing my patience and after several warnings I eventually had to hand him a yellow card. Just a warning however but a clear signal that I would have to see a big improvement in his work or else he would be in danger of losing his job. His duties were basically that of a waiter/barman with responsibilities for serving guests and looking after the dining room and keeping it tidy. Also he was expected to help outside when we were quiet with guests and join the guys in their daily chores to keep the lodge and gardens looking the best. This area was where Erenst particularly fell down and I found him skiving off a few times and taking the soft option. Anyway the yellow card didn't work as instead of doubling his efforts he chose to walk and didn't pitch up for work the day after I spoke to him. I gave him an opportunity to change his mind as I was really worried about his chances of getting another job and felt he needed to be busy or else he could go astray. But unfortunately he took the first available lift to town and I was torn between feeling sorry for him and feeling relieved as he was beginning to affect morale. We did miss him off the football team as he was an exceptionally good athlete and skilful ball player -probably the best player we had. The staff were not displeased however which was interesting and in fact more information emerged after he was gone about how others had been covering for him. Martha though was very upset and insisted that Erenst had not been treated fairly. She just wouldn't accept that he had been given every chance. The situation was further complicated by Anthony's friendship with Erenst as they had hit it off well and had become quite close. Martha now started creating problems and I waited for a reaction which duly arrived a few weeks later.

Occupancy at the lodge was still pretty low at this stage and I was trying everything I could to bring in more business. I was constantly on the phone to operators and agents promoting the lodge and spreading the word locally in an attempt to fill rooms until the tourist season really took off in August. What was encouraging was that the guests we did have were still extremely positive in their feedback regarding the facilities and service and many promised to return with their friends. This was especially uplifting when guests had been travelling right throughout the country staying in the best lodges and still Ghaub compared favourably to all the others. I began to seriously consider spending some time in Germany as one cannot ignore the fact that over 50% of our guests are German. We also had training recently from an accountant lady friend of Andre who introduced us to a new pastel system with detailed accounting which makes our book keeping system more efficient. We are still waiting for our new credit card stamping machine and a second phone line which would makes things much easier. At the moment we still can't receive phone calls if we go online which is a nuisance. Andre has suggested offering a sheep to the guy at Telecom which could see us move significantly up the waiting list for a second line! This is how things get done here at times but it's important to remember who you should offer what to! We are making a little extra money by selling souvenirs at the lodge including key rings made from the stone inside a Marula fruit which is carved out skilfully with the Ghaub logo and room number on them. I buy them in Tsumeb from a local entrepreneur called Eddie who could sell sand to the Arabs! There is an Eddie in every town and any visitors to Namibia will come across them and enjoy the banter as they try to make a sale. Usually they will accept half their first offer.

I forgot to mention that last time I was home I nearly didn't make it back as I was almost arrested at Gatwick airport under suspicion of been an international terrorist! One of the partners had asked me to bring back an animal injecting gun for the farm as apparently there was nothing like this in Namibia and it would make the farmer's job of dosing the cattle much easier and quicker. I have to say that this thing looked just like an automatic machine gun with stand attached. Security at Dublin were not impressed but allowed it to travel in the hold but when we got to Gatwick, London that's where the fun started. I was waiting with Anthony at the carousel and was approached by a very official looking security officer who enquired as to our names and asked us to follow him to his office. We weren't quite under arrest but were certainly under suspicion as he asked us to explain the contents of this poorly wrapped gun like object! He turned out to be reasonable about it however and once there was no ammunition for the gun he let us proceed! Another lesson learned and an international incident avoided.

As an avid Newspaper reader when at home I really do miss my daily paper. You can't exactly go round the corner for the morning Independent to peruse over a leisurely breakfast which has always been one of my little pleasures in another life. There are a few local papers that I get once a week which can be quite entertaining without meaning to be. There was a heading recently which caught my eye in The Namibian on the front page, 'Man asks Judge for his gun back in Murder case'. You couldn't make it up! The problem pages are a riot as well. Another heading caught my eye recently as well in a Dear Frankie type page, 'My partner wants to see other women, should I trust him to be faithful?' You have to smile sometimes. I notice on a serious note that the situation in Zimbabwe is receiving a lot of comment and the local journalists are very critical of the stance taken by both the South African and Namibian governments for not speaking out against Mugabe's tyrannical rule. Each week in the Namibian there is a top ten section around the world which relates to achievements that deserve worldwide recognition. Well Ireland finally got a mention last week and we made no 1 which I was initially very chuffed about until I read that Ireland is the leading producer of rubbish per capita anywhere in the world. Even the United States is ranked only at No 3. Charming!

I attended another funeral this month which was very different to my previous experience. It was possibly the first time that I felt really uncomfortable since I have been here and obviously in the wrong place. It was the passing of a sister of a woman I met at the local Bank in Tsumeb. This lady had been very helpful to us more than once and when I heard her sister had passed suddenly I thought I should pay my respects. The deceased was aged 32 years and apparently had a serious drink problem. The congregation were all well to do black people who seemed well off as the clothes and jewellery on display were unlike anything I had witnessed previously and there was an air of formality about the proceedings. I definitely received a few curious looks as one of only two white people present which eventually spooked me a little. The service was very Gospel like and there was a young organist/singer who I have met subsequently leading the celebration of this lady's life. (He works for Nico at the auto works/car repair garage in Tsumeb.) I slipped away after the church part of the service ended instead of joining the mourners as they walked the short distance to the nearby cemetery. I just felt uneasy and clearly there are times when you need to know your place and on this occasion I wasn't welcome.

I took a trip to Windhoek recently for some meetings to promote the lodge and to pick up some supplies. Leaving before dawn at 5.30am. I watched the sun come up in my rear view mirror as I headed South West. That time of the morning is magical and I haven't lost the feeling of absolute wonder as I pass the four hour drive with Van Morrison, Nanci Griffith, Luke Kelly and John Prine for company! I have been listening to much more music here as I have no television and long car journeys give me an ideal opportunity to listen to my eclectic tastes. I return to my old favourites usually and I suppose I am a country boy at heart. (I got a buzz one night recently when one of our guests recognised the opening bars of a Steve Earle tune coming from the bar claiming to be a big fan. At last I found another one!). The trip is fruitful as I call into Air Namibia to enquire about our corporate rates which we were promised. Turns out however that it will not mean cheaper fares as we only qualify for late cancellation rates but no real savings. I pop into Avis as well which seems to be the most competitive car hire option. I have subsequently found a company called Odyssey which offers far better deals. Make sure you get unlimited mileage cover however if you are coming as you can end up paying a lot more otherwise. I am becoming more streetwise when it comes to dealing with suppliers and have had plenty of experience in price negotiation. I can be ruthless enough when necessary and refuse to be taken advantage of.

Even the bad days are manageable as there are always some compensations. The wildlife is certainly one and I could never tire of watching animals in their own habitat. You can go several days and see very few animals and then suddenly you are surrounded by them. Sometimes when you look out first thing in the morning you will see the vervet monkeys crossing the lawn on the lookout for an early morning snack. They prefer berries and fruits mostly but would take any scraps of food around the bins. I brought Anthony out for a late night drive a few nights ago in the hope of seeing something new. It was very disappointing as we only saw pairs of unidentified eyes in the long grass but no positive sightings. A stronger search light would be helpful. Then just as we made our way back to the lodge feeling a bit deflated a leopard crossed the road in front of us and made our night. My first cat after five months but well worth the wait. I thought at first it was a stray sheep until I noticed this large bushy tail. Our most frequent wild visitor to the garden is a young duiker which is a member of the deer family. The staff call her Dookie and tell me that she was reared around the lodge years ago and never strays too far away. Although not tame she will allow guests get quite close and she is our star attraction for now. Bono, our pet mongrel plays chase with her sometimes and it really is the funniest sight. I watched one of the farm hands driving one of the tractors past the lodge one day as Dookie was chasing Bono across the grass and he nearly crashed the tractor he was laughing so much. The farm workers are busy at the moment working with the cows as it's the calving season. They are using the fields next to the lodge as they have a good system and deliberately keep the cows close to the lodge at this time to guard against predators. We have had forty two calves born so far and expect at least twenty more in the next two weeks. It is quite a sight to see more than forty young calves together in a small area calling for their mums! The guys have also dosed and treated the calves born six months ago and it was interesting to watch this operation unfold. The grass is all cut now and we have at least three hundred large bales stored for later in the season.

We have also had a new addition to the staff recently as Christine Berg arrived from Germany for six week work experience. Christine's parents are friends of a friend who asked us to take her for a stint. She has some good catering experience which will help as she is studying food and nutrition at university in Germany. She has also been involved with horses all her life and I am anxious to use her experience to good effect as we begin to develop our plan to provide horse riding trails for guests. All we need now are some horses and some gear as we are starting from scratch! Reminds me of an old friend from Walterstown football days Eamon Ward who once became very enthusiastic about wind Surfing and rang me up once to tell me he now had all the equipment except the board! Surely that's the most important piece I replied! It's like taking up golf and getting all the equipment except the clubs.

Recently we arranged a get to know you week-end at the lodge when we invited some of our neighbours and some new friends that I have met locally since I arrived in January. It was a way of saying thank you as in one way or another as all those invited had been helpful to me as I struggled to settle into my new home from home. Included were the local Doctor from Tsumeb and her family, a couple from the Bank in Grootfontein, the lady from Avis and her children and a couple who supply us with all our cleaning materials. In all we had fifteen adults and seven children as our guests and it turned out to be a very enjoyable relaxed couple of days. The company was great and I learned lots about the local history and it was interesting that most of the adults had been to Ghaub as children with their own parents. Seemingly before the lodge opened it was a popular farm to visit because of the history and opportunity for hiking and mountain walks through the farm. I believe that the week-end will ultimately bring in business as they all promise to return with their friends and I plan to have more of this type of meet and greet week-ends for friends when we are quiet with touring guests.

I am becoming intrigued with the people here and their customs. Black Namibians are typically proud people, hard working and extremely loyal in my experience. I admire their strength of character and their attitude to life and it challenges something within me to reconsider my own priorities. I love their acceptance of each others differences and their apparent willingness to follow their own traditions and beliefs while allowing others to do likewise. I am aware that superstition and fear of the unknown is however an issue for many. I hear the staff speak among themselves about evil spirits and ghosts and they seem to believe strongly in astrology and horoscopes. For me there is a conflict between their faith in believing that their life is mapped out for them and still they are convinced that there are spirits at play that can upset their plans and dreams. When I travelled one week-end to the coast I was inundated with requests to bring back sea-water by most of the staff. They explained that sprinkling sea-water around your house wards off evil spirits and helps to cleanse the atmosphere. So remember that the next time you are in Bettystown or Brittas Bay! I also enjoy and admire the different fashion styles here which vary from tribe to tribe and their distinguishing hairstyles and head dresses. On any given trip to town you often meet the Herero women out walking with their colourful dresses of several layers with matching coloured hats shaped like a matador's. The Damara women are less colourful but have amazing hairstyles which are not always flattering. They seem to be very fond of wearing these badly fitting wigs and extensions that can look very odd and they seem to change their hairstyle every few weeks. You can be caught out at times unable to recognise someone you met previously as their appearance changes so dramatically. Even among the staff the Damara women seem to be in competition sometimes to see who can come up with the most unusual hairstyle! You can also spot several women carrying their shopping home from town balanced on their heads looking very graceful. Their elegance and poise is remarkable as well as their strength. The men are typically dressed in darker colours and they can be seen walking slowly through town in small groups. Everybody moves slowly. I notice that you rarely see men and women walking together. Sometimes women walk behind their partners rather than side by side. I still notice the routine and procedure for organizing a lift as no matter what time you pass through a town or village here there will be pockets of people sitting under trees in the shade as they wait for a 'hike.' I would find that extremely frustrating not knowing when you might get home or reach your destination but it just seems to be accepted here as the norm.

I took delivery of seven new chickens last week that travelled all the way from South Africa at a cost of N$51 or five Euros each. We now have seven white South African hens and seven brown Namibians sharing the same coop. So far relations seem friendly and cordial. The Namibians though have to get up to offer their seats when the South Africans want to sit down. Only joking! So far they seem to be getting on well and we are now producing fresh free range eggs every morning for breakfast and I have to say that I get a great kick out of it. You can still clearly see and taste the difference between the eggs we buy in town and our own. It's another item ticked off from my must do list which I put together earlier in the year.

The building at the staff quarters is progressing but is painfully slow and my patience is been stretched by the absent foreman! To add insult he produced a quotation recently for nearly three times the originally agreed price and I have to admit I lost the plot. Granted we did ask for an extra room to be added to each house as well as the new bathrooms and showers but this was becoming ridiculous and another challenge to my newly acquired business negotiating skills. I point blank refused to pay the money demanded and considered closing down the whole operation there and then. We reached an impasse which got worse when his boss got on the phone and threatened to come out to the lodge to get his money one way or the other. It really got nasty and I had to call on Andre to negotiate on our behalf as it was getting out of control. We found agreement eventually but it left a sour taste and confirmed for me that builders are without doubt the same all over the world! Always hidden extras and promises of I will be round tomorrow to finish that job but tomorrow never comes!

I had hoped that after five months here I would be proficient in Afrikaans and perhaps pick up a little German. In truth however I have failed miserably in both. I have started to speak a little Afrikaans and the morning is probably the best time to get me! There are about ten different ways of greeting someone in the morning and an exchange can last several minutes with little grunts and sounds added for effect. German is more difficult but I will try to force myself as it would certainly help at times. In reality everyone speaks such good English that you don't really need to push yourself.

Had an interesting visit last week with Anthony to the Cheetah foundation in Otjiwarongo which is about a two hour drive away from the lodge. It was a spur of the moment decision and as we were quiet after a busy week and so we took off for the day. It turned out to be very interesting and fascinating to see cheetahs in captivity up close. There were eight or nine young males that had been reared by the foundation which seemingly could never be released into the wild as they would never survive. We were there for feeding time and got some good photos which I will treasure. Anthony loved it and is considering working as a ranger at some stage which would suit him. His three month stint was coming to an end and I was really proud that he adapted so well to the challenge and had worked hard for the duration of his stay. He missed his friends at times but found the experience of living in Africa for three months very rewarding. I genuinely believe that this will stand to him and he will return home with a different appreciation of what is really important and it will help him to follow his own dreams. Just maybe he might have a different appreciation of his old man as well.

7

IF YOU WANT THE RAINBOW YOU HAVE TO PUT UP WITH THE RAIN

Despite the emphasis on the business and the work I always believed that I was privileged to be getting this opportunity at this stage of my life. I had described it more than once as a lifestyle choice as well as a business opportunity which in hindsight may have concerned my business partners just a little! There was an element of fate and destiny about it and at times I felt that this was part of a great master plan put together by someone else. Just maybe Mum was looking down on me and still trying to use her influence to make things easier for me again but this time I wasn't fighting with her. We had so many of those conversations over the years when I had asked her to allow me make my own decisions, choose my own friends and make my own mistakes. It used to drive me mad and I wished she wouldn't interfere so much in my life. When I began doing the same with my own kids I understood her a little better. You know you are getting old when you start turning into your parents and I would have some of my Dad's personality traits as well. Heading towards 50 I suppose I was more open to the possibility of such a drastic lifestyle change that I would never have considered in previous years as the children would have been too young and would probably never have done it at a later stage of my life as it would have been too late and impractical. But now it seemed right and possible and I thought I could do this. Was it just a middle age crisis or the search for a distraction away from the mundaneness of an ordinary predictable life.I could appreciate the attraction in revisiting my biking days by buying a Harley and taking to the road but it never really felt like I was looking for an escape. I wasn't particularly unhappy or restless and in fact had no complaints about my lot. Family life was good, work was challenging but still rewarding mostly and I had my interests and hobbies. No real financial pressures and no desire to jump on the back of the Celtic Tiger. At the same time I did carry a longing of sorts for adventure and was open to the possibility when it did present itself. Without Marian's blessing it would never have happened though. She would hate to hear me say that but it's true and not everyone's partner would agree to their husband taking such a step and essentially take on the responsibility of looking after three demanding teenage boys. Yes I would be home on average every three months for two weeks and they would come out to Africa for a month during school holidays but it was still a huge change for the family. I think it's fair to say too that the lads adapted really well and played their part on making things easier for their Mum. They really responded well and tried not to create any problems for her. I worried about all of them and missed them terribly at times and as mentioned that first spell away was just awful. The boys took on more responsibility which I think made things more manageable for Marian in my absence.

I was even more determined to build a future for us and could concentrate on the work knowing that the family were doing fine. I believe it was having so much time to think that proved to be so significant because it allowed me time and space that I never really had before. Sometimes too much time is difficult and can play tricks on you. Long drives alone without the distraction of a working radio or CD player on never ending stretches of open road can be enjoyable but raises some challenges too. I found myself fishing in the past and not always appreciating what came up in the nets! School days were revisited and all the old insecurities replayed lifted by the occasional moment of euphoria by the recall of a forgotten moment of success or shared joyful episode. I became quite deep in my thinking at times which bordered on melancholy which could drift into madness if I allowed it. I found myself thinking back over events in my life when my reaction to certain situations was unreasonable and out of character. For example I used to get very irritated whenever I went to the cinema if people talked or made unnecessary noise around me. There was one occasion in Stillorgan in Dublin years ago when a guy next to me left his seat when the film was just about to start and returned moments later with a cooked meal of chicken and chips under his coat. I couldn't believe it as the smell was quite strong plus the fact that he was making a racket. I could sense Marian beside me anticipating a reaction and encouraging me to let it go. I couldn't hold my tongue and turned to him asking him was he seriously going to have his dinner there and then next to us. I suggested that he move seats quickly before the film started. He could have been a psycho in hindsight but luckily he accepted his fate easily. He actually turned to me and asked in a slightly confused manner could he come back to his seat when he was finished! I have actually retold that story many times against myself. I had a few experiences in Namibia when guests especially tested my patience. But my mindset continued to yoyo and my moods rise and sink especially when alone on the road. Mostly I remained in control of it but there were times when I was happy to pick up a hitch hiker for company and a bit of distraction. At these times I was aware too of moments of extreme clarity, moments of inspiration and creativity that I was unable to access previously. This became a common enough experience which I believe was encouraged by the surroundings and the sense of freedom I felt within. Perhaps this was part of the personal journey and further evidence of the layers that lie within us perhaps if we take the time to explore them. Namibia had a wow factor and Africa wove a spell but I could resist what was happening to me or willingly stay on board and see where it would take me. The following couple of months were to prove to be just as inspiring with the usual mix of highs and also the odd darker moment.

I returned home in early June with Anthony after a whirlwind three months. This time was different as I had company and we had now shared something that will stay with us for a very long time. I feel fortunate to have had the time with 'Anto' as we worked and lived closely side by side in a strange setting and it brought us closer together. It helped me to review my role as a parent and again I didn't always like what I discovered about myself. I thought basically I had made a bags of being a father over the years and had wasted an opportunity that I could never have again. Like everything else I suppose nobody goes to parenting school and we make it up as we go along influenced by our own experiences growing up. It's a wonder that there are not more problems as really there is little preparation for one of the most important roles in life and anyone can apply. You try your best but rarely get it right and I suppose I tried to make it safe for the lads to bring their problems home which I believed was one of the most important traits a parent can offer. Instead I think now I was so rigid and strict that the lads were probably afraid to raise anything important in case I over reacted. I used to imagine that Anthony was up to all sorts when he was younger and convinced myself that I was failing him somehow. I wanted what was best for him but didn't know how to provide it. Only Marian's solidness and reliability kept all the lads on track and again she forced me more than once to have a good look at myself. We survived the teenage years without too many problems but this time away was good for both of us. I realised quickly that I shouldn't have been worrying about him as he was essentially a well grounded young man with the same insecurities as me. In fact I now believe I was up to far worse when I was his age and certainly cannot put myself forward as a suitable role model. Having the time together meant that we chatted more than ever before and spent days together sharing the delights of the country. I probably gave away too many secrets as I shared some of my own early misdemeanours which he is now quick to remind me about when it suits him. When I used to give him a hard time about smoking he was able to bring up my own disclosure of smoking at the cinema in Ardee all those years ago before I reached my 12th birthday. Big mistake to have ever mentioned that. There were other stories too of mitching from school, making gunpowder at Halloween and crashing my Dad's car into the garage door which Dad took surprisingly well! So maybe I was no angel and hardly in a position to preach. Overall I feel the experience brought us closer and will remain with us. I am pleased that he was there for an important period of time as the business evolved.

The two weeks at home were filled with catching up with family and friends and doing a little marketing of the lodge. It's a strange feeling to meet up with everyone and try to describe what Africa is like as words cannot replicate the experience and beauty of the place. We have made plans for Marian and the two younger boys Christopher and Gareth to come out for the month of July. I am becoming a frequent flyer and compiling air miles at a rate. It never becomes a hassle and each journey brings something different. I have met some very interesting people in queues at airports over the last year and in fact have offered invitations to total strangers to visit the lodge which some have taken up. I can safely say that I am more content at this stage of the venture than before as I look forward to really sharing the experience with Marian, Christopher and Gareth. Perhaps this time is best captured by the reports I sent home for the months of June and July.

'Christine, our German guest is settling in well and proving to be a popular addition to the staff team and a help in the kitchen and dining room. I really wanted to take advantage of her experience with horses too so we decided to try to find a couple of horses for the lodge. They had to be the right kind of horse at the right price as funds were tight and if the horses were unsuitable for guests no matter how well bred they were it just wouldn't work. We visited a few farms after making a few enquiries locally and I met a young Namibian girl who believe it or not worked in Ireland at one stage at a racing stable in County Cork. Jana worked in Ireland for about a year for work experience also spending some time on a stud farm in Sligo. I eventually spoke to a guy in Otjiwarongo, not far from the cheetah foundation, who had a couple of horses for sale and we decided to head off early one morning in the hope of finding a suitable horse. We borrowed what can only be described as a crate which we placed on the back of our old open backed pick up van which was our new horsebox. Christine never saw anything like it but Jana assured us that it would be fine and that was how horses were often transported here. We eventually found the farm and the owner was a very pleasant white Namibian who doubled as a Doctor at the local clinic! I would have needed a camera to capture what next took place as after lengthy negotiations and choosing a nice looking eight year old chestnut mare with Christine's help we were unable to persuade the horse to get into the crate. After much shoving, pushing, cajoling and brute force we had to admit failure and drove all the way back with an empty 'horsebox.' Jana and Christine went back two days later with a proper borrowed box and returned with Charmaine who has a better temperament than her new owner! We then bought a gelding off Jana herself called Wrinkles, a six year grey Arab and a good looking strong horse. We paid less than N$11,000 which is less than 1,000 Euro for the two horses which was good value and certainly considerably cheaper than you would pay for the same type of horse at home. Now we were up and running with two suitable well trained horses but no tack, gear or equipment. I had cleared out one of the garages at the lodge and planned to turn it into a tack room for all the gear I was planning to buy and the horse feed etc. No need for a stable as the weather allows the horses to remain outside all year round. There was a funny incident around this time too when I asked Tato (pronounced like the crisp) to return the borrowed horsebox to his owner. He is usually very reliable, willing to help and readily agreed as I couldn't afford to be away from the lodge for the best part of another day. On the way he was stopped by the police and his licence did not allow him to drive on the main B1 motorway to Windhoek. The policeman had been standing out in the warm sunshine all morning and agreed to let Tato pass in exchange for the cool drink he spotted on the passenger seat! It could only happen here. There have been other examples of fine waiving since I have been here since my first encounter with the traffic police. A small bribe can sometimes be agreed but you have to be careful not to offer an inducement to the wrong person. Mika was stopped in Tsumeb recently for not wearing his seat belt in town which can mean a N$300 fine but the policeman suggested they could talk about it. Mika explained he only had N$100 and this was readily accepted. One of our friends from Avis was telling me recently too that she was clocked doing over 200 Kilometres an hour which could find you in jail and your car impounded. But $150 Dollars later and she kept going on the long road to Katima! Driving is indeed one of many pleasures here and the country should be seen by road. The surfaces are good mostly and with so little traffic you can drive at speed. Animals are the biggest problem and night driving can be hazardous. Kudus and warthogs often cross the road and sometimes the Kudus will actually move towards the lights. I have so far glanced off one warthog and nearly hit a cow standing in the middle of the road coming from Windhoek recently. Lots of people I have met have been involved in serious accidents with animals so be careful if you are planning to visit here. The countryside is beautiful though and a typical drive towards the coast can take you across what looks like three different continents. You could easily imagine you are travelling across Nevada, into the Northern territory in Australia and then through Southern Spain in the same afternoon.

Arriving back from Ireland we travelled back to Ghaub directly and Marian and the boys finally got to see the farm and lodge properly for the first time. On the first Sunday we went to the Maria Bronn School as I was anxious to share that experience with them. It didn't disappoint and the service was as entertaining yet very spiritual as any I had attended. The children danced their way to the altar with the gifts in a rhythmic choreographed routine which was captured on camera by my Scottish friend Alan Hendry. Alan is a very gifted photographer who runs a media business with his German wife Gesa in Windhoek. I have asked him to do a promotional DVD of the lodge and to help us set up a new website. It is possible to view the images at *www.ghaub.com* and you can appreciate the quality of their work.

We also did some travelling when the family were over and visited some other lodges to compare notes. I made some good contacts and picked up some helpful hints on how to improve our standards of service. I can now recommend some nice lodges and put an itinerary together for anyone who wishes to travel to this beautiful country. Our favourite lodges were The Vingerklip Lodge, The Rostock Ritz and the Africat foundation at Okanjima with their cheetahs, leopards, lions and wild dogs. We also drove back to Solitaire in the South which we loved again and Marian and the boys spent a week at the coast in Swakopmund while I was busy working. It's not all plain sailing though but if you want the rainbow you have to put up with the rain. What great philosopher came up with that nugget? Apparently it was Dolly Parton! You do still get the occasional guest at the lodge that is impossible to please. We had a German lady recently who complained that her room was too big! Another complained that her tea was too hot. It really is hard sometimes not to do a Basil Fawlty! I just have to smile sometimes and count to ten. We also had a visit from a Vegetarian hunter recently! You couldn't make it up but it's true and we received a call from a neighbouring lodge requesting four rooms at short notice due to an over booking on their part. We were happy to oblige as we had rooms available but the guests turned out to be American hunters who only wanted to talk about all the animals they were hoping to shoot! It wasn't easy as there were other guests that night who were anti-hunting and there were a few interesting exchanges in the dining room during dinner. But to cap it all one of the Americans refused meat as she was vegetarian. On the plane back from London last time I noticed that there were a lot of hunters dressed to kill! I thought how ironic it was that half the plane was coming to view wild animals in their natural habitat while the other half were coming to their best to shoot them for sport! I have decided I am definitely a conservationist but only after experiencing hunting at first hand recently. I decided I should try it once before making any judgements as I have met some enthusiasts here who do not strike me as gun totting extremists with a nose for blood! Andre is one and he offered to take me out early one morning around the farm as we needed some game for the dining room.

We headed off at 5.00 a.m. as the sun was coming up on a cold crisp winter's morning. For a full hour we drove without one sighting of anything that would be considered suitable for the kitchen. Eventually I actually spotted a fine male specimen Kudu with large antlers standing alone grazing some seventy yards to our left. Pointing to Andre in hushed tones he took aim from the back of the buggy and this incredibly loud bang rang out. The Kudu dropped instantly and we hopped off and rushed to inspect the prize. Andre had managed a clean hit to the shoulder and apparently the perfect shot which means no distress to the animal and no damage to the meat. We managed to winch this incredible large member of the deer family onto the back of the buggy and I have to admit I was not enjoying the experience. Shortly after this we came across another pack of female Kudu which were difficult to spot as they seem to blend into the background. Another successful clean hit and we had bagged enough meat for the lodge for the next three weeks. Nothing will be wasted and I am reassured that it is necessary to cull the Kudu herds regularly to keep numbers manageable. Overall I am happy to have witnessed hunting up close at least once but it's not something I would want to repeat. I am a conservationist at heart and I just couldn't personally take down one of these beautiful creatures.

I should mention too that since last time I invited the nuns from the Maria Bronn School to visit the lodge for Sunday lunch recently. I wasn't sure they would accept as I thought that they may have a vow of abstinence or something which might prevent them leaving the convent but as it happened they were delighted to accept and in fact it seemed to lead to an internal conflict as to who would travel and who would stay to mind the house! In the finish we had five sisters, Bernard the English professor who I became friendly with and a driver and all arrived like a bunch of excited youngsters let loose for the day! Sister Lidwina, the head sister, led the party and there was a relaxed informality to the afternoon. After lunch we went on a farm drive and came across lots of animals and there was plenty of banter and good natured joking among the gathering. It was one of those moments that stand out for me as there was a crossing of cultures and backgrounds which were easily bridged and language was not a problem despite our differences. My admiration for the dedication the sisters have for their work grew even more and the simplicity of their lifestyle is remarkable. I think they thought I was a bit odd and eccentric. They certainly found out a lot more about the Emerald Isle.

I have been thinking a lot lately about my standing with the staff and my role here as a foreign employer in their country. I struggle with it at times as they are so willing, obliging and hard working and never question my position. We pay them more than the going rate and have tried to improve their working conditions and their accommodation significantly. Like most people they would prefer more but are happy to be in employment and in a position to send money home to their families. When I am in town shopping I never feel uncomfortable even when I am the only white person in a shop with 100 or so black people going about their day. You take your place in the queue and greet everyone civilly and it's all very normal and relaxed. I don't experience people looking up to me or down at me and it feels like there is an accepted equality even though I would stand out in the crowd as being European. I don't believe that my being here is to someone else's disadvantage and I think I would pick up any tension if it existed.

We took delivery recently of our new staff uniforms which look very smart and give the staff a new identity. I notice already that when we go to shop in town with the staff they like to wear their uniforms as it shows they have jobs and there seems to be a level of status and respect for anyone working at a local lodge. We have a special shopping day at the end of each month when all the staff has a choice of two days to do their monthly shop for essentials and stores for the coming month. Initially it used to be a full day and I found myself hanging around killing time waiting for all of them to return when I should have been busy at the lodge. I noticed too that some of the staff were having a few drinks and spending too much of their pay on non essentials and basically using the day unwisely.

When I came here first I remember I was in Grootfontein o Friday morning to pick up some messages and as I arrived town the place was buzzing with a real carnival atmosphere. I asked a white shopkeeper what the occasion was as it looked like a national holiday or feast day. 'You must be new here', says he, it is pay day! This became a monthly event as the last Friday of each month was a day to avoid town if possible as culturally pay day means party time and no consideration for the rest of the month. That is definitely a feature here as with many of the local people there seems to be a tradition of spending when you have it until it runs out and then do without until next pay day. Some employers insist on paying their staff in the middle of the month instead or twice a month to avoid families having to go without. I will often be asked for an advance or a loan and had to quickly learn to say no or else become a soft touch. There is an element of desperation at times and lots of people will ask for money but usually they will not push it if refused. There are very few examples of public begging typically although tourists are targeted in the towns for loose change. Maybe I am no longer seen as a tourist which explains why I don't get this type of attention. I am getting to know more local people and usually meet a familiar face when in town. I still buy souvenir key rings from my contact Eddie and sell them on to guests. It's interesting that Eddie will always find me when I am in town as there seems to be a local network system when news travels quicker than phone calls or text messages! I had to have a word recently with one of the farm hands that was approaching our guests selling his handmade crafts and trinkets as they climbed on to their coach early one morning. It just looked wrong and instead I now sell them at the office and give him the full price instead.

Soon my good friend Allen Moran and his family from Ireland are coming over to visit and I am looking forward to sharing the experience of Namibia with them. I worked with Allen in another lifetime as we soldiered together as child care workers in the juvenile detention centre in Finglas, Dublin. It was certainly important then to know your friends as we were often outnumbered by out of control youngsters and unfortunately landed with colleagues who would run a mile at the slightest hint of trouble! We can laugh now but at the time it was tough work and there were days when you just had to live on your wits. I could always rely on Allen and we have remained in regular contact over the years helped by our mutual interest in Gaelic football. My sister Evelyn and her husband Ian are returning too for their second trip to Namibia this year in August and I have plans to take them to see a few new lodges. I have started to do a bit of cooking with mixed results but at least I am learning to be a bit more adventurous in the kitchen. The farm is busy and we now have 135 calves born over the last six weeks and it is quite a sight to see them all in the pen together looking the picture of health. The harvest is two thirds way through and very interesting to watch up close. We are averaging about three tons per hectare which is pretty good without irrigation. We have had no rain for three months now and it's getting warmer during the day but still cool after dark. It is winter after all!

I missed seeing Padraig Harrington win the British Open Golf for the second year in a row and just read about it three days late. I would have given anything to be sitting in front of a large flat screen watching the last 9 holes live on the Sunday but I suppose that is a small sacrifice to pay for choosing to be here. As I write Bono is sitting at my feet, the sun is warm in a cloudless sky and the birds are singing. Three large warthogs have just wandered into the garden in front of me and there was a pack of Vervet monkeys playing in the trees behind me earlier. Sights and sounds that you won't experience on an average Saturday afternoon in South county Dublin. No I am quite content with my lot right now and there are more than enough compensations for all I am missing at home.' Now if I can only convince Marian to move!

8

IF YOU LOOK FOR IT YOU WILL FIND IT, IF YOU DON'T IT WILL FIND YOU!

The number 23 enigma concerns the belief that all events are connected to this number. The earth tilts on a 23 degree axis. It takes 23 seconds for blood to circulate around the body. Julius Caesar was stabbed 23 times. There are lots more. Well I have a few of my own. My only sister was born on the 23rd June.1982 was a very significant year for me for many reasons. I was 23 at the time. The registration of my first motor bike was Jzu 23.So far so good. Well on the 23rd August 2008 I came very close to doing myself a serious injury. I shall explain what happened shortly but suffice to say that my enthusiasm for horse riding took a knock. I was again alone after Marian and the boys went home at the end of July. I knew I would have the next two months to pass and it felt like a long stretch without the family and with not a lot to look forward to. We were expecting the month of August to be busy with guests and there was a growing list of things to do before the real tourist season kicked in. You needed to be in good form and well rested as there would be many sixteen hour days ahead. In truth as it happened I was lucky to be able to walk! I had always wanted to be around horses and approached riding with great enthusiasm as this was a great opportunity to make up for lost time. Initially I was careful and started riding out a couple of days a week although walking out would be a more accurate description of what took place. I started going for hikes down the farm with Lotto, our most experienced pilot, and always chose Wrinkles, the quieter and better trained of our two new horses. No problems at the beginning and I progressed from a walk to a canter and to a trot without too much difficulty. After about four weeks we started to gallop a little and I was enjoying it as

I had no problem with the speed from my motor-cycling days. Balance was another matter however and I suppose it was inevitable that I would have a spill at some stage as I was beginning to think this was easy. One Sunday I went out for some reason and chose the mare Charmaine just to test my skills. Well she clearly recognised that she had a beginner on board as she made a bolt for it and took off down the field at a rate of knots. I hung on for as long as I could and should have eased myself off and settled for some lost pride but decided to stay with her and try to bring her under control. Big mistake as she veered sharp right at speed and I went sharp left landing in a heap on the hard dry ground. Lotto came to check how I was and was unable to suppress a big grin at my misfortune. I knew I was in trouble and could hardly move as I was both winded and very sore at the base of my back. I struggled to my feet and felt sick and faint but tried to put on a brave face. Turned out I fell on my coccyx and I imagine now came within a whisker of a serious spinal injury. I was black and blue for two months and partly out of cowardice and partly because of lack of opportunity I didn't get it properly checked out. It took a full six weeks before I knew I was ok but had lost all my enthusiasm for horse riding. I did eventually get back up but never regained my confidence fully and I suppose in the words of my uncle Martin it takes forty years to get forty years experience! I will stick to motorbikes from now on as at least you can pull the brakes when you want to slow down. It could have been worse I suppose and I now have a healthier respect for jockeys and riders who make a difficult job look easy.

Time moved on and the weather changed again. I was thinking that the job of a weather forecaster in Namibia must be one of the easiest jobs in the world. "Tomorrow will be extremely warm with good sunny spells and clear skies." You would never be wrong and you can just expect the same the next day. I was hearing about flooding at home and struggling to imagine how an Irish Summer could be worse than an African Winter! One difference here is that the local people love to hear and see the rain falling and I am slowly beginning to understand why.

August has been our busiest month so far at the lodge with guests and the Italians are here in numbers. We have had more guests in one week than we had in a month earlier in the year. Most of them are friendly and easy to entertain. There are always some however that you can never please no matter what you do for them. I actually find some of the guides are more difficult than the guests and sometimes they act like they own the place and make unreasonable demands. Most groups with more than four people employ a guide to show them around and these are usually German/Namibians or Italians who act as drivers, translators and tour leaders. Some of them are used to pushing their way and are rude and unreasonable. I have to remind them that they are also guests when they come to stay at Guest Farm Ghaub.

I had one particularly difficult situation to deal with recently which tested my ability to reason with the unreasonable! When I had been at home in June for a short break we had a booking for a group of fourteen German guests for two nights from one of the established tour companies. This company have been good supporters of the lodge since I have been here and they would have be highly regarded within the tourism trade. The only difficulty I had experienced with them previously had been in relation to the attitude of a couple of their guides. Most of the guides are excellent -hard working and professional in their manner and kind towards their guests but there are the exceptions that seem to think that they are the most important person in the group. On this occasion when I was absent this guide a Mr Fritz who is known as an arrogant, pompous individual gave Mika a very hard time and led a chorus of complaints about the service and particularly about the price of our wines. Now the quality of service and attention to detail is usually first class and our prices are extremely competitive compared to neighbouring lodges. I cannot remember receiving a complaint like this since the beginning of the year so I decided to look into it. Having spoken to all the staff and making a few enquiries through some of my contacts in the business I concluded that a) the staff had done everything possible to provide the level of service we expect on this occasion and b) Mr Fritz was a trouble maker, a bully and a bore who tried to take advantage of the locally managed lodges. I was really annoyed and decided to contact his employer and explained that I would not accept that type of behaviour at our lodge and asked his boss to relay to him that I would be happy to discuss our prices and our service when he next returned to Ghaub. I knew that the company had another booking later that month which Mr Fritz was due to lead. The owner sent back a prompt reply of apology and was in full agreement that Fritz had been out of order. She was in fact very positive about Ghaub and had been receiving very complimentary comments from her clients recently regarding the lodge. She more or less intimated that he was a bit erratic in his behaviour and would speak too him at the earliest opportunity. On August 14th Fritz arrived back at Ghaub as expected with a large mixed group of sixteen guests consisting of Germans, Austrians and Swiss tourists. The bus arrived on the dot of 3.00pm as usual (typical German efficiency) and the driver was clearly on edge. He brushed past me abruptly and greeted Mika like a long lost friend even though he had been extremely rude to Mika last time. I made a point of introducing myself and suggested that as soon as his guests were comfortable that we should have a chat. He was more interested in heading for the bar but again I had to impress upon him that we needed to talk first. I insisted on calling him Mr Fritz for the duration of his stay. He gruffly made reference to the letter I had sent to his boss and we had a heated discussion on what had actually taken place on his previous visit. His biggest gripe seemed to be the price of our Rose wines which he felt were exorbitant. I went through our price list with him in detail and he reluctantly accepted that perhaps he had been out of line and I received a luke warm apology. I felt that there was no point in taking it further and we settled down to make the most of his visit. Later that evening when he was on his second bottle, (which was part of the problem), and as I was clearing some glasses in the bar he was singing to entertain his guests who were clearly unimpressed. Now how many German singers can you name?

Exactly! As I passed through he broke into what can only be described as a vague version of "When Irish eyes are smiling" and was clearly trying to needle me. Without thinking I turned around and said "Mr Fritz, never forget that if you make friends with an Irishman you will have a friend for life, but if you cross him he will never forget you" and kept going with my overloaded tray! Maybe I went too far but I felt he needed to be put in his place. He is unlikely to forget the stubborn contrary Irishman who could be even more unreasonable than himself!

There is another lady guide who I initially had some difficulty with but eventually we got on famously. Helen, another German, has been a regular over the years and is well known to the staff for her slightly eccentric behaviour and for the unpredictable requests that she invariably demands. She typically insists on getting the same room for herself and usually drives straight past reception without checking in. When she also visited this month our first problem was that her room was now my room and I had no intention of moving! Since I arrived I have stayed in one of the guest's room as Mika has lived in the house at the lodge for years and I didn't think it was right to take it over on my arrival. We will need to eventually build more accommodation but for now I was happy enough to use the guest room which happened to be Room 1 which is the closest to the lodge. On this occasion Helen arrived mid afternoon and true to form drove straight past the front office and down the path to the rooms before placing her own bags at the door of Room 1. I gave her a few minutes and then met her on the path looking a bit flustered. I introduced myself as the owner and welcomed her and her guests to Ghaub before inviting them all to check in at the office to collect their keys and join us for a welcome drink. Helen's routine was upset and she wished to unpack first. I told her Room 4 was ready for her and again she struggled with the change but went along with it. As it turned out after that we got on famously and she was an excellent thoughtful guide who put her guests first. We had a good chat after dinner and she was very complimentary about the direction the lodge was taking. There was an eclipse of the moon that first night and as a keen astrologer Helen was in her element as she insisted on turning off all the lights around the lodge to witness this rare phenomenon. Apparently it will be several years before this happens again and here in the Southern Hemisphere the stars and galaxies are incredibly close and clearly visible. It is another amazing feature here and real star gazers and enthusiasts are in their element.

During the month of August my good friend Allen and his family arrived from Ireland and spent five days with us at the lodge before heading off on a two week adventure to explore the delights of Namibia. Allen is from Mayo originally but now lives in Galway with his wife Mellie and two sons. We followed similar paths in our careers and have kept in touch over the years since our days in Finglas. They were great company and his twin boys Rory and Colm helped me feed the animals early each morning. Typically Allen wanted to help and ended up leading a work party one day and spent a full day of his short holiday painting the staff houses. It looked like a very professional job and was much appreciated. He also gave me a quick lesson in making proper Irish Coffees one evening and we have since been offering them to our guests on a regular basis. Allen's wife Mellie was great company too and I must say that I am happiest when friends from home are here sharing the delights of Namibia with me.

I had another surprise recently when I received a phone call one afternoon from a local looking for accommodation for the night at short notice. He sounded Namibian and I guessed he was an Ovambo from the North West. When I asked him his name he replied Sean Sherlock! I couldn't believe it and said without thinking that he didn't sound like a Sean Sherlock! 'No he is here beside me and I am his driver', came the reply. He must be Irish I thought and sure enough when the driver passed me on to his friend I was speaking to not just any Irish man but a well known Labour politician from County Cork. I am not sure which of us was more surprised to find a fellow Celt in the back of beyond but Sean quickly agreed to call in and ended up staying three nights with us. We had great chats and typically realised that we had some mutual friends at home. It nearly always happens when Irish people meet abroad they invariably know some of the same people. Sean is one of the youngest deputies in the Dail or government and was working on a fact finding mission to Namibia He had been visiting and supporting the work of the Overseas voluntary organizations particularly the programmes working with Hiv and Aids victims. Clearly Namibia was making quite an impression on him. Sean had originally been hoping to go to Mongolia and had been somewhat disappointed to be given Namibia when the countries were been allocated. Now however he had no regrets and had been blown away by the country and the reception he received everywhere he visited. He was winding down now with a few days off before returning home and it was by chance that he called the lodge here. We discuss Irish politics long into the evening as well as the current recession that I have been hearing about. Sean promises to return and I really think he will as he seems to have been bitten by the Namibian bug.

Life is never boring here for sure and each day brings a new challenge. We keep two cows at the lodge now for fresh milk all year round. Three weeks ago one of our cows broke her leg as she stumbled on her way into the paddock. Billy arrived down from the farm to do the needful and a loud bang echoed off the mountain behind the lodge. Two days later I was up at the farm collecting game meat for the kitchen when I spied our old friend hanging up in the cool room with her head on a shelf looking at me! It's a bit disconcerting looking at the cow you were milking a few days previously now hanging from the roof of a fridge. Billy actually offered me the head which I declined! The list grows.

Erenst's mother Martha, our second cook had also walked out suddenly last month and left us in a bind. I wasn't completely surprised as she wasn't getting on with the rest of the staff and always seemed unsettled since her son left us. But I found a new cook in Tsumeb through a friend and Johanna is now settling in. I have also taken on a new barman/waiter and another lady for the laundry and rooms as we were getting busier. I think we now have a highly motivated hard working staff and the atmosphere among the team is even better. There does not seem to be any tension between the staff members and this is crucial that they can work easily together. Mika continues to amaze me with his attitude and ability to pick things up so quickly. The guests are always mentioning him especially in our guest comment book and really he is one of our most important assets. I hope he stays with us as he clearly could work in any lodge and has been sounded out more than once. He seems to be very loyal to Ghaub however and wants to remain here for the long term. He did forget his son's birthday recently and his ex partner was very annoyed with him and gave him a right telling off. It just proves that people are the same around the world. Men forget things and women over-react!

We had some return guests recently which is always a good sign. One Dutch couple with two children left on a Tuesday night on their way northwards and returned on the following Saturday for two more nights. We suggested that they join us for a visit to the Maria Bronn Sunday service in order to sample a Namibian treat. The school children treated them like film stars and were convinced they were Brad Pitt and Angelina Jolie! We also had a very friendly German couple who also stayed for two nights on their way to Victoria Falls in Zimbabwe. On their way back they had a reservation about 70 Kilometres from Ghaub in a rustic lodge which is popular with some guests. They checked in and checked back out within half an hour as they didn't like the look of the place or the antiquated décor!

I am still coming to terms with Namibian protocol and procedure and have had a few challenging incidents recently. It is often when trying to carry out a simple banking transaction that the system seems to break down. I wanted to pay a bill to another lodge where Marian, myself and the boys stayed for two nights last month. I couldn't use my credit card for some reason and watched as the teller withdrew N$ 4,348.00 from my account counting it out slowly and deliberately from one drawer before placing it straight back into the same drawer when the paper work was completed! I also often have to wait twenty minutes or longer in the bank in Tsumeb when I want to withdraw petty cash for the lodge. Sometimes I lodge N$8,000.00 and want N$2,000.00 for cash and they have to call head office in Windhoek for clearance. Even though I know most of the staff by name at this stage and have handed over four times more than I am asking back it remains a frustratingly lengthy process.

August 26th was a national holiday here celebrating Heroes Day. Shops close down and lots of people take a long weekend to celebrate. It's a bit like St Patrick's Day at home and an excuse to party. I read a piece in the local paper condemning Namibians for using these celebration days just to drink and there are lots of examples of alcohol fuelled incidents reported around the country. I asked a few people who the heroes were that were been remembered and nobody seemed to know!

When travelling to and from town I will almost always meet people hitching for a lift and usually laden down with bags and sticks and all sorts of odds and ends. Sometimes I will stop and sometimes I decide to keep going as you have to be careful who you stop for. I stopped on the road last week on the way back from Grootfontein for a middle aged man on his own who was waving me down frantically. I decided on this occasion to stop and as I was driving an old open backed buggy and offered him a seat in the back which he gladly accepted. It wasn't until he was climbing in that I realised that he was seriously under the weather. He held on to his few belongings closely and when I let him out ten Kilometres down the road he needed help to climb down out of the buggy. I suggested to him to be careful not to spill his luggage and he gave me the best gap toothed grin as he stumbled off smiling to himself.

The animals are more noticeable around the lodge this month as it's getting warmer and food is scarce in the bush. The vervet monkeys are now regular visitors in the garden most evenings just before dark and I think they are watching the cats. The staff tell me that the monkeys would take them if they could as they are still quite small. The warthogs are getting more cheeky and now come right up to the rooms after the grass that has been watered. One of the staff Lotto spotted a herd of Eland down the farm last week when exercising the horses. They are the biggest member of the antelope family and are beautiful creatures to see up close. I was sitting out under the veranda at my room late one night recently having a relaxing cup of coffee and listening to the night African sounds. Suddenly a little barn owl landed at my feet and stood there for a full minute just staring up at me occasionally swivelling his head 360 degrees. It was an incredible sight to see one so close and I thought he might have been injured until he just took off and disappeared as quickly as he had arrived. The bird life around the lodge generally is incredible and we had an Australian lady staying recently who was a keen bird watcher and she was blown away by the variety and amount of species she had spotted in one afternoon. She in fact recommended that we should be marketing the lodge as a bird sanctuary for true enthusiasts. We had an interesting request from a local guy who runs a small garage and panel beating business in Tsumeb. He has helped us out a few times since I have been here and when guests have a problem with their cars. Nico wanted to go hunting on our land and offered to hand over anything he managed to bag. Unlike most hunters Nico uses bow and arrow and describes it as a pure form of hunting. I really wasn't sure but I decided to give him a chance as long as he kept well away from the lodge and didn't interfere with the guests. He arrived back three hours later with two large warthogs in the back of his van looking very chuffed with himself. As it was getting dark I suggested he keep one and we would put the other one in the cold room. But a fully grown warthog is a large and heavy animal and as we struggled to lift him in through the kitchen door suddenly there was blood everywhere and I lost the head! It wasn't going to work so we put the warthog back in the buggy and had to begin a major cleanup operation before the guests arrived back from a trip to the cave. It was another lesson learned.

The hard work is beginning to pay off and the business is beginning to grow noticeably. Through word of mouth the lodge is receiving a lot of favourable attention locally and we are building up a nice reputation as an affordable family lodge with excellent service. It is very satisfying to hear the guests speak so positively about their stay and compare Ghaub with the more expensive exotic lodges that they have also visited. Once we have our new website up and running I am hopeful that we will see a noticeable growth in our room occupancy. The leading operators are now back supporting Ghaub after a few quiet years. We are included in many itineraries put together by the big companies as they try to showcase the country to European visitors especially. We are having Germans of course but also many Italians, Swiss, Austrians and British guests. Usually there are older couples but sometimes families with young children who are easy to entertain and usually are settled down for the night before 10.00pm. Your body clock has to adjust here and I am now in a regular routine of sixteen hour days seven days a week but enjoying it mostly.

I am missing the family hugely and if I wasn't so busy I think I would crack up sometimes. I have resisted getting a television and in truth wouldn't have time to watch it. I missed the Olympics completely apart from five minutes one morning when I had to call down to the staff quarters and watched a Czech lassie win the javelin and the fancied American relay team drop the baton in their final. Only just heard that Padraig Harrington added the PGA to his British Open title and now has won three major golf championships which is an incredible achievement.

The cost of living here is only a fraction of what it is at home. The other day I had a coffee, a cool drink and cheese roll in a nice café in town which cost N$24.00 or two Euros. Newspapers are 30 cent, cigarettes two Euros for 20, and cans of beer less than a Euro each. Your money goes a long way and makes it cheap for tourists. The expense is in travelling here but otherwise it's possible to arrange a life changing holiday here fairly reasonably.

The farm is going through a quiet spell after the finishing of the harvest about two weeks ago. We eventually ended up averaging 3 tons per hectare and close to 500 tons in total. The national average has been 2.2 tons per hectare so another result for Billy. Most of the maize was sold nearby in Otavi and we held onto about 100 ton just in case the price increases in a few months. More rain in March would have boosted the yield substantially but Andre and Billy are pleased overall. The seasonal workers were let go this week as there is not enough work for them which is a pity as most of them are hard working and were eager to stay. They could be re-employed later in the year when the calving season starts again in November.

Eyelyn and Ian have been with us again and seem to have fallen under the Ghaub spell. My friends Rita and Mary from the Rutland are planning to come over in October and my cousin Siobhan and her husband Pat are coming out soon for the cricket and will also visit. The Irish are certainly beginning to make an impression on the locals and I think we share the same lust for life, happy disposition and good humour unlike many other Europeans tourists.

I spent last evening after dinner playing chess with a German Doctor from Munich. He had very little English and looked a bit like Hannibal Lecter. He spent the game chatting away in German and I hadn't a clue what he was saying. We were still able to communicate however and I let him win as he was drinking Chianti all night! I find it hard to believe that I have been here for close on eight months at this stage. It has been the most incredible time and I can only describe it as the best and yet the most difficult thing I have ever done. Would I do it again if I could turn the clock back? Absolutely.

9

MEA CULPA

There have been many personal conflicts that I have faced since I arrived in Namibia. The experienced has tested my resolve on many occasions and challenged my previously held beliefs on a variety of issues. One of those issues concerned the question of smoking and I think it's time to come clean once and for all.

For years in my role as an addiction counsellor I believed that nicotine should be included among our list of primary addictions which the Rutland offered treatment for as well as alcohol, drugs, gambling and food. To me tobacco has always been the most addictive substance and the one that affects most Irish people. My own history with tobacco is quite an interesting one. My first memory which I will share is untypical and difficult to believe. Actually I have an even earlier one which I had almost forgotten. Believe it or not my first cigarette was aged eight years under the covers of my parent's bed early one morning. I wasn't alone either but as the older brother I can hardly lay the blame at my younger brother Stan's feet as he was only six! Back all those years ago it wasn't unusual to have a male baby sitter and we were looked after by a young Bank official one evening as my parents had a rare evening out. I think his name was Mr Mc Fealy and I can't remember very much about him except that he left his cigarettes behind. Next morning early I had this mad idea of trying out this smoking lark and lit a cigarette off the small electric bar fire we had in our front room. Sneaking back to bed I was puffing away when Mary Mooney from Croghan Hill, the family minder, (sounds like we needed a lot of minding) came down the hall enquiring what the smell was. The two culprits covered themselves under the blankets which only made things worse and we had to come clean. Mary to be fair was reasonable about it apart from threatening to tell Mam and Dad as soon as they returned from their daily mass. In their wisdom they decided to teach me a lesson which would put cigarettes out of my head for good by inviting Mr Mc Fealy back up after work to collect his cigarettes. My next memory is going outside to dig up the said cigarettes that I had buried in the soggy garden earlier that morning! Total embarrassment for me and you would think it might have put me off cigarettes for life. I suppose in hindsight the lesson was learned till I reached the age of eleven. By then I was a confirmed social smoker and recall smoking at the cinema in Ardee with my best friends one night when we all had bought ten Calumet each! I think that was the name although they are a long time off the market. Funny I could remember that and not recall a simple verse of Irish poetry! Anyway at that time I was buying cigarettes in ones and twos for two old pence each and sneaking off around the woods nearby to indulge my habit. It's the fact that I was smoking alone that surprises me most now. I suppose football took over and sport in general and smoking took a back seat right through my formative secondary school years. While others in my class had a quick drag between classes in St Finian's I had no interest but I suppose I was just on a break! Then when leaving school at seventeen I rediscovered the urge and smoked on and off for three years even though I was playing football at a competitive level. During my time in Child Care College I made a pact to quit with a friend Noel Mc Mullen and we stopped one Christmas and in truth it wasn't that difficult. I was cheating however as I continued to have an odd cigar when on holidays, after a big match or when fishing for some reason. I could stop for several months, smoke during a two week holiday abroad and then stop again. That continued for about twenty years although I was never comfortable smoking in front of the family. Mostly I would disappear and smoke alone which took me away at times and therefore it became too unsociable. Then at around forty I decided I was ready to stop once and for all. I figured that when you reach a certain age it's time and we only have a certain amount of smoking in all of us before risking our health. I know it's part denial and part delusion! Then of course when I started working in the Rutland Centre and became more familiar with different addictions, cravings and withdrawal my awareness of the power of nicotine increased. I willingly joined up with the anti-smoking brigade and became a typical former smoking bore that secretly criticised others including close friends for their lack of will power. I volunteered to lecture the clients on smoking cessation and often shared my own relationship with tobacco and how I had conquered it. I challenged the myths around smoking and encouraged the groups to include tobacco in their quest for sobriety and a chemical free future. I was finished with smoking and it never caused me a thought. That was until July 2008 when I relapsed and willingly and knowingly picked up the weed again after a long absence. I could blame lots of factors and find a convincing reason why I returned but in reality I would be only fooling myself.

During the first part of my first year in Namibia I became conscious of the numbers of local people and guests who smoked here. It was like Ireland years ago before the smoking ban with Restaurants, Cinemas and Bars full of smoke and it felt quite strange. I had become used to smoke free zones and was in fact proud that the Irish were quite pioneering in their attitude to smoking cessation in the workplace and public areas. Who would have thought that we would embrace the ban and that people would stick to it, especially in pubs and bars in rural Ireland? Even devoted smokers were largely in agreement that the ban was working and that it was a welcome development. Now in Africa it was like going back in time and it was the white people more than the black people that were more obvious in their smoking habits.

I began slowly to be fascinated watching people smoke in the bar at the lodge and gradually began to see the attraction in it again. Over a period of time I began to consider the possibility but not seriously at first. On long car journeys alone I thought smoking might make the journey shorter and less boring. Imagine. I struggled with the thought for about three months and then one afternoon in late August I stopped for a cool drink on the long drive to Swakopmund and bought a pack of twenty. It wasn't just any pack. It had to be Peter Stuyvesant for some reason even though I can't ever remember smoking them before. The power of advertising perhaps but no other cigarette would do. This was Africa and they were cool cigarettes and this was somehow going to make my life here even more complete.

The week before I stopped at that shop on the way to Swakopmund I had the bad fall off the horse at the lodge. I was really lucky and as already explained I could have been seriously injured due to my own lack of experience and foolishness. My back was killing me and I was still black and blue and covered in bruises which made driving uncomfortable. I could blame that fact but I know I was going to find a reason as my resolve was evaporating steadily over the previous month. I felt like I had a lucky escape and maybe smoking wasn't the worst thing I could do. Cigars held no interest either as I never really enjoyed them as they gave me chest pains sometimes. As I said I could find an excuse but there wasn't one and I smoked again because I could. It was a strange experience as I delayed opening the packet. Driving due west toward a setting sun the countryside looked amazing and I had a strange moment of contentment that life was good and that I had very little to complain about. Would smoking add or take away from that feeling. I can only describe it as like opening a present as the build up of anticipation was the same. I had to have a lighter too as matches would have taken something from the moment. The time came, I inhaled nervously and then again but nothing really happened. I was expecting a sort of dizziness or light headedness but it wasn't like that. I can't say it was pleasurable either, just strange. The cigarette felt small in my hand and I became conscious of the difference between the beginning of a cigarette and when it is half smoked. The feeling gets better and then the ending which is part ritual and part closure. I had a second not long after and again it was strange and vaguely familiar like a long lost friend. No feelings of regret or guilt however. No sense of what have I done after all this time. It took a few days to become familiar until I began to look forward to one. My insight into addictive behaviour and delusional thinking didn't get in the way and I was back. Over the following six months I continued to smoke except when I returned home for short breaks. I slowly realised what it was like to rush a meal in order to have a smoke. I also became aware that the first smoke in the morning was often the best. Initially I would put it off until after noon. Then it began getting earlier and earlier until I was having one at 7.30am with a cup of coffee instead of breakfast. The panic of running out also became familiar as there were times when we would not get into town for a week and I miscalculated my stash. Smoking the last cigarette when you knew you would have to do without was the worst. Nicotine does indeed play tricks and is a powerfully addictive substance and I would never underestimate the control it has ever again. I would also be a little more understanding and less judgemental of others who struggled to kick it and those who had no desire to quit.

When I went home and back to work in April I had already decided that I would not smoke at home for several reasons. I didn't want to smoke in front of the family. Sure I had given Anthony a hard time about his very occasional smoking only six months previously. I didn't want to go back to Rutland as a smoker too as I would feel hypocritical. I also didn't want to be considered a smoker at home. In Africa it was different for some reason. I could live with it here but never at home. Daft I know but that's me. I don't intend to smoke again unless I end up living in Namibia eventually. But never say never. Who knows?

It may not be a dramatic confession but it seems important to include in my experiences here. I still have no regrets which is significant. It happened but I am not beating myself up over it. Otherwise I can't say there is anything that happened during my time in Namibia that I would take back or wish to change.

Home thoughts from abroad

The year was flying and I was becoming more and more at home in Namibia. Every day continued to bring surprises and it was an education in cultural differences and customs. The Namibians are fine. It's the Germans I was having trouble with!

There has always been a close connection between Germany and formerly South West Africa. As a former German colony you notice the German influences in the architecture in Swakopmund and Windhoek particularly. Also the language is widely spoken and the place names have a German ring to them as well. It didn't take long for me to realise that more than half of the total guests coming to the lodge were from Germany. Looking back over previous years our guest books have several entries from Bremen, Munich, Frankfurt and other German cities. The lodge itself is steeped in history as it was originally a Rhenish mission back in the 1800s and we also have a German cemetery on the land with several casualties from the 1914/15 war buried there. I hate to categorise a whole nation but I am now aware that the Irish psyche and the German psyche are poles apart. Some are incredibly friendly and genuinely warm in their attitude and appreciation for the service they receive and the attention to detail. However I have to say that I have also experienced many with few social graces and no sense of humour whatever. They can be cold, arrogant and judgemental. In the service industry you will always meet guests that you cannot please no matter what you do for them. My personal favourites still include the German lady who complained that her room was too big and another who felt that her tea was too hot. What can you do in a situation like that? You really do feel like doing a Basil Fawlty type rant but you have to count to ten as the guest is always right. Well nearly always! We had another German gentleman who complained that there wasn't enough food during dinner after he had consumed enough for a small army! Another seemed to treat our Breakfast buffet as a challenge and confused us with one of those eat as much as you can for a fixed price establishments. You have to smile sometimes and take it although I did react a few times when I thought the guests were being rude or disrespectful towards the staff. At the same time I have friends here who tell me that German people are the most loyal, hard working and trustworthy race in the world and that once you make friends they are great company. Maybe I have been unlucky but for me the Italians and the Dutch are more like the Irish and have a similar sense of humour. The English are my favourites and I always look forward to their arrival when I see a group booking from Britain. Firstly they are stunned to find an Irishman out here in the outback. They are always interested in the story or how I came to be here and I have had to repeat it hundreds of times. I have to say I still enjoy sharing how it happened and of how Ghaub found us. Most English people are easy to please and are not looking for a problem. They are here to enjoy themselves and always seem to be comfortable in company or meeting with other nationalities. Perhaps it is the language that makes things easier for them but I suspect it runs deeper than that. The Irish and the English can be good company together and have more in common sometimes than we imagine.

During the month of September things were quieter at the lodge as expected. There was a steady flow of guests but not the same volume as the previous month. I actually managed to play a game of golf on a rare off day which was quite an experience. On a whim one Saturday after a busy spell I headed off with no clubs or equipment in search of a course I had heard about near Tsumeb about fifty Kilometres from the lodge. There seemed to be a flurry of activity as I arrived and the car was quickly surrounded by a large group of eager looking young black poorly dressed youngsters all looking to carry my bag. I recognised one of the bigger guys as a brother of one of the girls at the lodge and he introduced me to a guy called Charles who was organising the weekly competition. This guy could not have been more welcoming. He invited me to join his own fourball and use his clubs. So we set off as a fiveball and the other members of the group were equally welcoming. The game was very relaxed and the emphasis seemed to be on enjoying the company and less on the competition. We even had a lengthy stop for cool drinks after nine holes and there was no rush as all the other groups were doing the same. It was taking so long I had to excuse myself after thirteen holes and head back to the lodge to work as we were expecting a large group to arrive. The day was enjoyable and I could see that the caddies were all eager to play as they were showing off their swings every chance they had. I found out the following week we finished second in the competition as it happened though my own contribution to the team was minimal.

Not much time for golf since as there is always something to be done. Shopping in town is becoming a stressful event as you have to deal with many challenges and rarely come back with everything you wanted. I usually make a long list which grows significantly when others get wind of the fact that you are heading to town. All these opportunities have to be taken advantage of as it might be a week before anyone is going into town again. I typically have a long shopping list for Pick and Pay which is the local supermarket. I usually have to get diesel, petrol for the lawn mower, bottled gas, meat at the Butchers, stock for the bar, horse feed at Agra and some odds and ends at the hardware for the guys who work outside. You rarely get everything you need and I always seem to be in a rush to get back. Even though we might be quiet and Mika has everything under control I still put myself under pressure to get back for some reason as soon as I can. I will often have some passengers too which can slow me down as I don't like leaving anyone behind as they would have to pay a taxi over the odds to bring them back otherwise. If I have time I might have a coffee and a sandwich somewhere and watch the world go by for 15 minutes. It is always interesting as you see people going about their business and greeting each other in a typical African demonstrative way. When I rush back to the lodge expecting the place to have burned down in my absence or over run with unexpected guests I typically find that everything is under control and there was no need to be rushing in the first place. The worst part is when you are half way back and you remember something else that was needed. No matter how prepared you think you are there is nearly always something that you end up forgetting.

I still look forward to Sundays as it has become the highlight of my week. The nuns and the children at the Maria Bronn still give us a great welcome each week when they see the car arriving. It is becoming slightly disconcerting that I now have the mobile phone numbers of several nuns! Even the fact that they carry mobile phones I find amusing. The main reason I have the numbers is because regularly I receive requests that I might have work at the lodge for some of their relatives that are desperately looking for jobs. They are always interested in hearing stories about Ireland and Irish customs. I exaggerate just a little sometimes to make the stories more interesting. One Sister called Jacobina is very friendly and usually makes a point to greet the guests that we bring with us. One Sunday recently I noticed she was wearing a different habit to the other nuns. The Senior Nuns usually wear white and the trainees are usually kitted out in a bright blue uniform which sets them apart as novices. This Sunday Sr Jacobina was in a light grey outfit and I asked her after the service was it significant or had it a special spiritual meaning. She replied smiling that she had spilled tea all down her front during breakfast that morning and had to change quickly! I thought it was very funny at the time!

We are still having some very interesting guests to stay. You never really know who is coming and what surprises they will bring. I remember a couple from South Africa who were both in their eighties and could have passed for sixty. They were so fresh and full of energy and I was very taken by the fact that they were driving alone through the country. Great company and full of interesting stories about life in South Africa and how things had changed over the past twenty years. We also had a very odd Dutch couple who gave me the creeps! They actually looked uncomfortably like Fred and Rosemary West. They never changed their clothes while they were with us, ignored all the other guests and kept very much to themselves. My imagination was running wild and I thought they might be on the run or had escaped from an institution. They slipped away without saying goodbye too although they did pay their bill in full earlier. We also had a visit from Leonie, our marketing manager, and her family for a week-end in September and she was impressed with the changes we had made since her last visit in April during the tour operators week-end. The responses have been very positive from our guests to the tour companies in general. Most of the companies ask the guests for feedback and request that they score the lodges for service, amenities, facilities and activities. This helps them to grade the lodges and to recommend them for future tours. That's why I try to impress upon the staff that every guest is important and that we constantly need to upgrade. We have been encouraged to highlight again the bird watching angle as several keen bird watching enthusiasts are fascinated by the variety of species in the immediate surrounds of the lodge. The weavers are back too and are busy building their nests just in front of the office door. They are incredible to watch as they look like yellow canaries and the male builds the nest at the end of a branch having stripped the branch of leaves first. Seemingly this is to discourage snakes and other predators. Most importantly they build the entrance facing away from the branch which allows access only to other birds. The whole process from start to finish takes about eight hours and you can watch the males flying up and down with grass and twigs as they weave furiously singing while they work. Then when the male is finished the female comes to inspect his work and if the nest is not up to scratch she rejects it and he has to start all over again. Great isn't it! Women have the power again!

The animals generally are plentiful at the moment. Apart from the usual sightings we see the warthogs right beside the rooms most evenings as they seek out the watered grass. There is a large herd of Eland moving through the farm at the moment too. Beautiful elegant creatures that trophy hunters single out which I still struggle to understand. The vervet monkeys come and go you might not see any for a while and then they will be back around the lodge every day for a week. I am getting used to the sights and daily sounds that fill the air but never lose that sense of wonderment and appreciation.

The local papers are still full of interesting local stories that you would never find in The Irish Independent! One story caught my eye recently regarding the children of veteran soldiers who have been camping outside government buildings in Windhoek for the past month demanding assistance from the government. They don't seem to be receiving much sympathy. One senior politician when asked for his opinion on their plight was quoted as having replied "Just because your father was a Doctor and your mother was a Doctor it doesn't make you a Doctor-You still have to go to school." I am reminded constantly about the importance of family among the local people. Uncles and Aunts will often care for their nieces and nephews if their parents are absent for whatever reason. Grandparents also look after young children if their parents are working. When I was last home Mika's family had a celebration of his wedding which actually happened eighteen months ago. Apparently his wife's mother passed away six weeks before their wedding day and so they decided to have a smaller celebration out of respect. Now however his wife's family wanted to mark the occasion properly and relatives travelled long distances to be there. The problem was Mika was working as I was at home and we had to make a plan. I did my best to arrange a temp to cover for him and thought it would be possible but then they changed the dates again. Turned out that the party went ahead without the most important person and Mika's brother stepped in for him dressing up in full wedding gear for photographs! Hard to believe but absolutely true and apparently it is not that uncommon here for parties to take place without the host! I have also noticed incredible family resemblances here that you don't see at home. It must be in the black genes but brothers can be almost identical and children are often the absolute image of their parents.

The local music is a mix between hits from the eighties and local black rap artists. In most shops the piped music consists of golden oldies from another age. One restaurant in Tsumeb I mentioned before plays Country and Western music all the time as the owner is a fan but it sounds quite out of place here. I left in a few CD's which I liked including Frances Black, Mick Hanley and Nanci Griffith and the owner seemed pleased to add them to his collection. Whenever I was in town subsequently I would try to make time to have a coffee there and he would usually play one of the CDS when I arrived in. I have to say I got a kick out of hearing Mick Hanley in the wilds of Africa and I even heard one of the staff humming along to 'All the Lies that You told me' by Frances one day. Mick and Frances would be chuffed to know that they have a growing fan base in Namibia. The only Irish artists I see for sale here Foster and Allen, Westlife and Daniel O Donnell! They clearly have good marketing people working for them. When driving I still prefer Irish music as somehow it brings me closer to home. I imagine other Irish people working abroad also keep in touch with home through music. Van the Man for me is still the king and I am waiting for a film to celebrate his life and to recognise his standing internationally.

Around this time I was missing home and the family hugely. Marian was keeping everything going and really making this whole venture possible. I hope that it will ultimately secure our future and I will be able to pay her back somehow. There are times when it is really tough and the work is endless. It's not like a regular job and the hours are crazy sometimes. I prefer to be around as much as possible not because I can't trust the staff. It's just that guests like to meet the owner and it keeps everyone on their toes. Time off is rare but long days are worth it when you are receiving positive feedback from guests. It's hard to describe a typical day because there isn't one. But when we have twelve or more guests for example you are on the go from 6.30am until 10.00pm We don't close up until the last guest has retired for the night so it can be a long day on your feet.

Upon returning from home last time I had a very interesting experience at the airport. I travelled over with friends Rita and Mary from the Rutland Centre. I arranged that we would travel together and that they would spend five nights at Ghaub before I would let them loose to discover the delights of Namibia for themselves. Passing through customs I was a little nervous as my working visa had not come through. The lady at the visa office suggested that I just say I was on holiday if there was a problem. You are entitled to spend ninety days here during any given year without a business or working visa. I was well over two hundred at this stage but was lucky that the customs people had not noticed this before and I was able to travel back and forward to Ireland without a problem. Well this time I picked the wrong line to queue and I found Miss Conscientious who decided I was flaunting Namibian immigration rules and she intended sending me straight back on the next flight to London. I suppose she was really only doing her job. I made the situation worse by insisting that I was not working here as suggested by the visa lady and unconvincingly suggested that I kept coming back because I enjoyed the country so much. The situation was looking very serious as Rita and Mary were waiting for me inside arrivals and it was looking like they might have to make their own way to the lodge. I was embarrassed and shocked and really in a pickle. I decided to come clean and admitted that I was waiting for the visa to come through and that I was involved in a lodge in the North of the country and was hoping to bring employment and visitors to the country. They weren't impressed and couldn't care less what I was doing to introduce Namibia to a wider audience. I was now changing my story again and they were even more determined to deport me (if you can be deported from an airport)! Panic stations and alarm set in and I tried to call Andre in the hope that he could use his considerable influence in the country to get me out of this self inflicted mess. I was then informed that I would be sent back unless a working visa arrived at their office by 5.00pm that day. Meanwhile Rita and Mary were waiting patiently in arrivals for the fugitive to be released. As we had flown through the night they were amazingly supportive even though exhausted. The prospect of sitting on a plane for another ten hours back to London was not at all inviting not to mention the reality of having to abandon Rita and Mary. Eventually it took seven hours for the visa to come through and I was kept in a small room with the other 'illegals' which was an education in itself. One guy with no English spent the entire time crying and pleading with me to help him. He was from the Cameroon and as he had no money with him and no means of support he was going nowhere. I was in enough trouble myself and therefore not as sympathetic to his plight as I might have been on another occasion. I was just relieved when I finally got the nod after much grovelling and pleading which I felt some of the Immigration Officers were enjoying more than they should. I heard since that in a situation like this it is up to the individual immigration officer's discretion whether to allow someone pass through and the other officers would have given me two weeks to produce a valid visa. Seemingly the other officers all knew at 11.00am that I would be permitted to enter but my friend decided to teach me a lesson and keep me sweating! We eventually left the airport at 5.45pm having landed at 10.00am and headed for Ghaub with a quick stop off for dinner in Okahandja. I now was in possession of a three month working visa and had learned some valuable lessons. Be patient and always choose the right queue when chancing your arm or trying to enter any country illegally!!

After that things improved and Rita and Mary were great company for five days and they seemed to be very taken with the lodge and the country in general. We were also joined by my cousin Siobhan Nangle from Ireland and her husband Pat who had travelled over to follow the Irish cricket team in their tests with Namibia. The four Irish guests made quite an impression on the locals and even travelled to the Maria Bronn School together for the Sunday service. They were treated like celebrities by the nuns and the children and they were every bit as enthralled as I expected. They got some great photos and memories to take away with them from the experience. Mary and Rita, whom I renamed Thelma and Louise, headed off to Etosha on the Monday via the Uris lodge before heading for Swakopmund and the Skeleton coast. Siobhan and Pat headed in the opposite direction and as seasoned travellers the driving held no fears for them. By far the best times for me here personally have been when family and friends came to visit and it kept me going through the quieter times.

The language continues to be a problem only in the sense that I am learning very little Afrikaans and no German worth talking about. English is so freely spoken that you don't really have to make an effort to learn the local lingo. I do have some problems communicating as Irish phrases like "how's she cutting' and "Get up the yard" don't travel so well! The staff are doing really well and gave me a great welcome back as did Bono my shadow! The staff joke that I look after him better than them! Lotto has become very capable at looking after the horses and benefited from Ian's tuition and experience during his visit. Lotto is quick with most things except text messaging. For some reason he can't figure out how to send sms. In fact you could say that he took to text messaging like a duck would take to text messaging! As a former champion apprentice in Rhodesia many years ago Ian has lots of experience and I was delighted that he actually climbed back up after a gap of ten years to view the farm on horseback. The horses are in excellent shape and a local farrier who came to check them recently was very impressed with their conditioning. He actually said that Wrinkles, our six year old gelding was worth a lot of money and he would happily make us an offer. I ride out once or twice a week but in truth I never really went back with the same enthusiasm since my fall in July.

Andre has been to Ireland for a week and had a chance to meet all those involved in the business. He travelled quite a bit through the country visiting some farms and experienced Irish hospitality. I believe he even visited Burke's farm in County Meath where they make the delicious ice-cream. I can't wait to meet up with him and hear all about his trip. This was only the second time he had been to Ireland after a long gap and I know he has been blown away by the experience. Business is looking up and I took a very good booking for a party of eleven people for three nights in November for a work conference on a full board basis. It's a new departure for us and we are excited that offering work conference facilities will bring Ghaub to a wider local audience. Our website will be up and running soon but we want to get it absolutely right before we launch it. We have also ordered a newly designed brochure which will be a big improvement on my original rushed effort. Soon we have the Tsumeb Copper festival starting and we plan to have a stand to market the lodge locally. It's all go!

We had an incredible event here at the lodge recently which should be shared. I mentioned before that the staff were quite superstitious and have a strong belief in ghosts and evil spirits. Some of them came to me one morning to complain that they were not sleeping well and were convinced that there was a presence in their houses. They mentioned that they were woken by noises, sounds and shadows during the night which really scared them. As it was becoming a problem and affecting morale I decided to speak to the local priest I had befriended at the Maria Bronn school to ask his advice. He took it very seriously and admitted that he had similar experiences himself which really got my attention. Until then I was treating it a bit flippantly although the staff seemed genuinely scared. The priest offered to do a cleansing and a blessing of each house and when I suggested it to the staff they were all for it! The following Wednesday he arrived out with one of the nuns and the English professor Bernard who is quite a character and good company. On this occasion though he was very serious as he also had some uncomfortable unexplained happenings at his own house. It was quite unbelievable as the priest visited each house in turn followed by a throng of people in various states of dress and disbelief! All the children followed as he sprinkled holy water and burned incense in each room mumbling prayers in a language I couldn't understand. The whole operation took about an hour and was taken very seriously by everyone present even though I remained a little sceptical. However there hasn't been a word since and all staff are now sleeping peacefully so I have to believe that the restless spirits were reassured and are now at peace.

I forgot to mention before also that the former President of Namibia Mr Pohoomba actually came to stay at the lodge a few years ago. We found an old photograph with himself and Mika outside the entrance and I plan to have it enlarged and placed in a prominent area of the house.

The fashions and local style here continue to amuse and enthral at once. The hairstyles are still hard to fathom as the local girls still insist on wearing ill fitting hair extensions that look like they belonged to an older relative in another time. The white Namibian farmers wear ridiculous tiny denim shorts that make them look like Australian Rules footballers. I have to smother a smile when I meet them in the Bank and that's one example of local fashion I definitely won't be following. The Afrikaans women often dress inappropriately too for their age and it is not unusual to be surrounded in the supermarket by women that you would mentally put more clothes on.

I have been reading lots of books in my spare time and rediscovering the joy of a good read. Just finished a terrific book of interviews given by Bob Dylan over a thirty year period which really captured the genius of the man. He was writing songs in his teens that have stood the test of time but like most geniuses he is as odd as you like.

The surroundings here are still awe inspiring and breath taking. The people are proud, gracious and rarely complain even though they could. I met Lucas from the garage in town again recently and he still works twelve hour days, seven days a week with no lunch break and earns about One hundred and twenty Euros a month. But he was smiling and looking forward to payday. So maybe things are not as bad where you are as you think. It's all a matter of perspective.

10

WORDS ARE LIKE BULLETS.
WHEN YOU RELEASE THEM,
YOU CAN'T CALL THEM BACK

November was supposed to be a quieter month at the lodge and accordingly I decided to give some of the staff annual leave. Big mistake! Turned out to be an extremely busy month and in ways the most challenging since I arrived. More about that anon.

The start of the month is best captured by the experiences we had at the Copper festival in Tsumeb. This is an annual event that lasts four days and was described to me as a cultural celebration when the local people of Tsumeb come together to sell their wares and to meet up with their neighbours. I experienced it as The Ploughing championships, Puck fair and the Spring show all wrapped up together with a bit of Lisdoonvarna and St Patrick's Day thrown in as well! We had decided to book a stand to promote the lodge and bring in some local business. I arranged for the stand at a cost of around seventy Euros for the four days and we took turns to be present to meet and greet. We set up early on a Wednesday morning on what can only be described as the local Fair green. I had to go to Windhoek for two days for some meetings and to catch up with 'Thelma and Louise' before they flew home after their adventures around the desert. It was great to catch up with the ladies and although they hadn't quite driven over a cliff they had a few hairy moments along the way. They survived the journey and learned some valuable lessons, (never attempt to travel across three hundred Kilometres of Namibian gravel roads with no spare tyre was one!).We had dinner at a very nice Restaurant in Windhoek and compared notes. I think they will be back.

I arrived back on the Friday to take my shift at the stand in Tsumeb and the place had turned into Rio on speed! The Copper festival was in full flow with a real carnival atmosphere. Lots of dancing on the green to loud piped music and lots of drinking in the early afternoon sunshine. For me it typified the best and worst of Namibian life all at the same time. I was completely bowled over by the children dancing in small groups with no inhibitions as children would play football at home in the same setting. All of them were fantastic dancers with great timing and rhythm and they seemed to enjoy showing off their moves. There was one particular eleven year old boy who I recorded dancing on his own without a care in the world. He could make a fortune in Europe if he had a manager and a passport but in truth he will probably never have either. I was just sitting there agog until I couldn't help noticing that there were very few white people present. This was clearly a festival that the whites avoided. There was no problem however and I tried to blend in. Then around 7.00pm the live music began on the main stage and out of curiosity I decided to stay on just a bit to catch the start of the show. Just moments earlier two young women dressed the same had stopped at the stall and enquired about the lodge. I didn't pass too much remarks on them until they jumped up suddenly and joined the band as they were part of the backing singers and dancers and nearly missed their cue. The music was like a mix of Paul Simon's Graceland, modern hip hop with some terrific African rhythms. The dancing was out of this world and the crowd became very animated and joined in enthusiastically. The band were called Ndilimani and seemingly they are a political band made up of Swapo members and their songs are mostly about black civil rights. They would be the equivalent I suppose of the Wolfe Tones at home who I think have finally decommissioned their instruments! I decided it was time to get out of there but enjoyed the experience which was only somewhat sullied by the public drunkenness which I suppose is typical of the living for the moment attitude that is so prevalent here.

Mika had meanwhile timed his holidays well and he deserved every day he had off. He went home to his family in Ovamboland from the beginning of the month for two weeks but it left us a bit short staffed. We had a good booking of eleven people for three nights for a work conference from the Hope Foundation. We gave them a good inclusive price which they accepted quickly and I expected that they would be an easy group to entertain as they would be busy during the day. The best guests are usually the ones that you don't see. Another big mistake. They turned out to be very demanding and unappreciative in the main. They were a mix of Namibians, Americans, and Germans who worked together on a charitable project. The Namibians were to my surprise the most difficult to please and they were critical of the sleeping arrangements and the food. Local black girls that remained unfriendly and ungrateful despite all our efforts to please. In the end however the group did seem to get their work done and were more appreciative but it was a reminder to me of the demands of the service industry when you can never tell how your guests will respond.

Around this time the news of Obama's election was announced and widely celebrated throughout the country and Africa in general. In Kenya there was a national holiday to mark the occasion. I was chuffed to receive a picture of my nephew Tom with Obama's wife Michelle taken shortly before his election. Tom had spent several months in America supporting Obama on the campaign trail. I am delighted for him and more than a little proud. The picture is now placed centrally on the notice board in the office and draws a lot of comment from passing guests.

We have a new member to the Ghaub family as well over the past few weeks. The farm staff from Ganachaams found a young Eland up in the mountains and offered him to us as a pet. He is about five weeks old and a beautiful wild creature. We kept him inside for two weeks and bottle fed him which he quickly got used to. Now he rambles around the gardens with our two sheep and has become a popular attraction with guests. We call him Ndilimani after the cultural band we heard at the

Copper Festival. We are developing a pet's corner at the lodge which the younger visitors particularly enjoy.

One of the most striking features over the past month has been the arrival of the early rains. After six full months without a drop we had our first rain of the season recently which is unseasonably early this year. We had consistent rain for eight consecutive days which all the local people are delighted about. I still prefer the sunshine but there is something magical about this time of the year as the landscape changes quickly and there is a unique smell in the air. One farming lady I met described the rain as money falling from the sky! It means that the planting of the maize will begin on December 1st, a full six weeks ahead of last year. It remains warm despite the rain and the new conditions bring insects and creatures I have not seen before. The insects seem to get bigger and two nights ago there was a flying beetle outside the office door that was definitely the size of a small bird! I still haven't been bitten by anything thankfully and you do get used to the strange bugs after a while.

The month's highlight was undoubtedly last Sunday week when we had the children from the Maria Bronn School out to the lodge for the day. It was a carefully planned exercise that I promised months ago and we had agreed that it would only happen if we could bring all the children here rather than pick a small number and disappoint the rest. So when we had a quiet Sunday and Padraig and his wife were over from Ireland for a few days we went for it and put the plan into action. I had a quick lesson from Billy in the driving of the cattle truck as believe it or not that was our only means of transport. It could only happen in Africa but we managed to bring all three hundred of the children (and a few stowaways) in two cattle trucks with 150 girls in one driven by the handyman at the school and 150 boys with me. We set off on the 50 Kilometre journey over mostly gravel roads after an earlier than usual Sunday service. We got a few funny looks from passing cars but there was an air of excitement as the kids sang most of the way there. We were so overloaded that we had to fit 6 kids in the cabin of the truck with me and one of the staff. One of our passengers was about eight years old and had not a word of English. He was a member of the Tsan community which are really Bush people who choose to live in the wilds and survive by hunting and gathering wild fruits. He just sat there bemused by what was happening never changing his expression. As we got closer the singing got louder and the convoy arrived to be greeted by the staff who had offered to give up their day off to help out. As planned we divided everyone up into groups of fifty and gave them all a coloured wrist band made of wool and spilt them into six activities lasting one hour each. We had swimming for one group when another gang went horse riding. We also had football, treasure hunting, races and lunch as we couldn't possibly try to feed everyone at once. One group had to have lunch first which they were happy enough about. The previous day I collected bread rolls, soft drinks, boerewors which are like hot dogs, fruit and some sweets. In total we fed everyone for less than one Euro each and we had food over at the end. It was almost a loaves and fishes moment. The whole day passed off without a hitch and it was interesting that I didn't see one child crying or two kids fighting or arguing throughout the day. The nuns were a great help as well and there was a relaxed informality in their exchanges with the kids. Clearly the children feel comfortable, safe and relaxed in their company. Every hour I blew a whistle and everybody moved on to their next activity. I found myself looking after the treasure hunt and on the hour had fifty pairs of beautiful excited dark eyes staring at me as I read the first clue before they scattered off in different directions. I couldn't help noticing that even though there was an element of competition and a desire to win there was also a sense of team work and the older kids were watching out for the young ones. The last clue happened to be in the Ciunas room and so each time I sat with them explaining what Ciunas meant and told them stories about Ireland where I was from. They sat around hanging on every word fascinated to hear about another country ten thousand miles away and had lots of questions about Irish people and Irish customs. It was one of those special moments for me that I will never forget. Near the end there were nearly two hundred kids in the swimming pool at the same time as the order of events began to break down. Some of the group were reluctant to leave the pool when their time was up. The photographs are a howl. We had some prizes to give out at the end and it was noticeable how little cleaning up there was considering the numbers. Apart from the two sheep taking fright with all the noise and running back to the farm there wasn't a problem. We loaded up the two trucks for the return journey back to Grootfontein at around 3.30pm and the kids sang most of the way home too. It was a magical day with no hiccups and all arrived home safely. Not sure if we will rush to do it again soon but we might make it an annual event. Each Sunday since that I have been to the service the children have rushed to the car all excited talking about their day at the farm and asking when they can do it again. I am determined to help the school in any way I can as the whole experience has changed my mindset and restored my faith in ways I find hard to express.

It is always good to hear news from home although lately it seems to be all doom and gloom with talk of recession, job losses and bad weather. You can be removed from that here as the Namibian economy seems unaffected to date as prices for food, fuel and essentials are decreasing. Tourism continues to grow despite the cost of travel from Europe as more and more people discover the delights of the country. We have many returns at the lodge and it is not unusual for guests to come back year after year. I read recently that tourism is now the leading money earner right across the country ahead of agriculture and mining.

I am completely out of touch with the English and Irish soccer scene which is unusual for me. No time for golf either and that wasn't the best decision I have made to bring the clubs back out with me last time as they are now gathering dust in the wardrobe. I do envy some of my friends just a bit as I heard they are heading off to Spain for a few days golf shortly. There will probably be the usual debate over rules which are typically more Queensbury than Royal and Ancient! It's the craic as much as the golf that I miss. But there are more than enough compensations here. We have had a busy month again at the lodge with several nights booked out. One of the leading operators called Sense of Africa are really supporting us now and we are getting large tour groups who have the pick of lodges to stay in Namibia and Botswana. Andre brought some farming friends to stay for two nights recently and some of them are involved in the hospitality industry. We did a lot of driving around the farm and they were all interested in the maize and cattle and the land generally as you would expect. I am still working sixteen hour days at times and there isn't much time for relaxing or sun bathing I can tell you.

You still see some strange sights in the course of a given day. Always expect the unexpected here is a good motto. I was pulling out from a fairly upmarket hotel in Windhoek last week after a meeting, when the security man at the gate was sitting there busily picking his toe nails with one shoe on and one off! He gave me a big salute as I drove passed and carried on gardening. You also often meet on the road guys on bicycles carrying sticks and logs to bring home for the fire or for sale. It defies gravity how many sticks they can manage to fit on a small bike. All you can see is what looks like a small tree coming down the road against you on wheels! We were driving around the farm the other day with some guests hoping to spot some animals but usually you are lucky to see some Kudu, some warthogs and young deer. I am tempted sometimes to place large cardboard cut outs just out of range or stuffed rare animals high up in a tree just to impress the guests! This time however we came across a herd of sixty Eland wandering across the path around fifty yards in front of the buggy. It was an incredible rare sight and the guests were well impressed. There were three large bulls which were almost elephant like in size and they hopped the fence gracefully as if it wasn't there.

We are still hoping to take the staff on their promised trip to the seaside next month. I still struggle to believe that none of them have ever seen the sea but it's true. It came up in conversation during the year and I promised then that before the year was over I would take them for a week-end to Swakopmund. Time is running out and they have reminded me more than once.

I have been thinking long and hard about the future and at this stage I am considering staying here until next Easter at least. By then the lodge will be where we want it and I should be able to step back from it. I am missing the family and home hugely and realistically we are not going to be in a position to consider spending time here as a family at least until the lads are finished school. With things the way they are Ireland I cannot afford to pass up the chance of holding on to my job in the Rutland which will only stay open until April 2009. It will be so difficult to hand the reins over as I have become very attached to the lifestyle and the people here. The staff are now more than colleagues and we have built up a good working relationship that is mutually respectful. I notice when I visit other lodges that there is a noticeable divide between manager and staff and the owners play a very peripheral role. For me I think it's important for the guests to meet the owner and they expect and appreciate the chats we have as we share our experiences of Namibia. The rewards are seeing the business build and to hear the positive reaction of 95% of the guests.

I still have to get my visa renewed as I don't want a repeat of my experience last time at the airport. Trips to Windhoek have become easier as you get accustomed to the long drives and I still have Steve Earle, John Prine and Van Morrison for company. It takes a little over four hours on good roads with very little traffic. Windhoek itself is a surprisingly modern capital city and very interesting to visit. It has some excellent shopping centres that would compare with anything we have in Dublin. It is described as the cleanest African capital city in some travel books and you can appreciate why. I like to watch the people pass from a central coffee shop as there is such a mix of interesting styles, fashion and colour. More than 90% of the people are black but there is no difficulty for whites or tourists to mix and shop as long as you are mindful and respectful.

I am still called Mr Gerry or Master Gerry in some instances which I struggle with. Despite encouraging people to drop the

Mister or the Master they seem to prefer to keep that formality and deference which has become ingrained in their psyche.

Virtue is better than wealth (Kenyan proverb)

It seems appropriate at this stage to try to describe some of the more personally challenging times during my sojourn in Africa. Along with the moments of clarity and deep contentment there were also moments of dark despair. My moods were swinging and changing like the wind at times and I had difficulty trying to explain why. I think it was partly to do with the time spent alone and the challenge of been left with your own thoughts with no distraction. Always for me personally the most difficult times have been when I have too much time to think and nowhere to hide. I become insular and introspective and start to wonder about the meaning of life and what serenity is really about. I read somewhere that this country is a massive vacation for the mind -that time for soul searching abound. The surroundings can inspire and bring you on natural trips as strong as any drug. Maybe it's the come down and the withdrawal that confuses.

I found myself at times talking to myself which is bordering on madness although I never answered myself back! Was I really happy here? Could I be happier? When do you know that it doesn't get any better? Long drives alone were the most difficult before I got the radio fixed as there was a thin line at times between appreciating the natural beauty of the landscape and wishing I was back in the real world. I think it was partly to do with missing the family so much and also feeling like a stranger in a strange land. It does feel unreal here sometimes and yet more civilised than the so called civilised world. It brought me back in time and my dreams were like flashbacks of a previous life. The clarity of those memories and feelings was stark and not always comfortable. All my old self doubts and perceived failures returned and I would wake suddenly convinced I was back at school thirty five years ago. Now it feels like a cleansing of the soul and a moving on of sorts. Just maybe I have caught up with myself. I can now grow into the person I always knew

I was and wanted to become. I can feel at ease in company and find my voice. I have something to contribute and have achieved something with my life which seemed beyond reach. It's like an itch that I couldn't scratch. A deep rooted longing that could never be satisfied by natural means-until now. Maybe it will inspire somebody to follow their dream. Just maybe someone will be encouraged to think why not rather than I could never do that.

What was it really all about? Was it just a gap year at fifty and a mid life crisis of sorts. Was it just a business venture and an opportunity to secure our future? Was it more than that and a part of someone's plan for me? It did always feel a bit predetermined as if it was meant to happen. From the first day I arrived here at Ghaub I genuinely felt it found us. There were too many coincidences for it to be any different. I almost recognised the place and although it sounds farfetched I sort of felt I had arrived home. Maybe a reward for some good deeds in the past. Maybe just a stroke of luck but whatever the reason it has been a privilege and best of all it doesn't have to end yet. I really don't know what the future holds but I do know that my life will never be the same again whatever happens.

Sunday service at Maria Bronn

Just some of the happy kids at the school

Just one example of the wonder of the Ghaub cave

*Gerry, Mary Reynolds, Audrey Tallon, Chris and Mary Glennon
cross the Tropic on the way to Solitaire*

Life on the farm as the harvest is in full flow

Healthy calves just 2 weeks old

The staff dress up for church

A curious mix of cultures

Meet the staff

Hilma, Ida, Frieda, Johanna, Christofine,
Andreas, Mika, Klaus, Martin, Immanuel, Lotto

Mika Shapwanale

Christofine Dei- Geis

Ida Dei Geis

Frieda Gawas

Immanuel (Tato)Muteto

Martin Shinyala

Johanna Frans

Lotto Haufiku

Andreas Likuwa

Hilma Kangili Mbuale

Klaus Ndjamba

II

NINETY PERCENT OF POLITICIANS GIVE THE OTHER TEN PER CENT A BAD NAME!

The best way to share the real experience here for the best part of fifteen months is to return to the monthly log I kept which was intended only for family and some close friends. But the story evolved from that and best captures the progression of the work and the growing number of new experiences that emerged. December 2008 and January 2009 I tried to summarize together as I had returned home for Christmas around December 19ᵗʰ and returned on January 9ᵗʰ for what was to become my last stint here for now.

"At this stage I have spent all of 2008 in Africa with occasional visits home. It has been memorable and challenging but mostly a privilege. The people here are incredible and their spirit and attitude to life is commendable. I have got to know the staff at the lodge as friends and colleagues. I miss them when I return home and receive a warm welcome when I come back, usually with some small Irish gifts. The smallest present is much appreciated and the thought is definitely what counts. They are all interesting characters in their own way and have had incredible lives before they arrived at Ghaub themselves. I would prefer to introduce them all at length but it would take forever so I will instead give a brief description of the current lodge team instead.

MEET THE STAFF

Mika Shapwanale

Mika is perhaps the real hero of the story. Originally from the far North of Ovamboland he arrived at Ghaub ten years ago as a young man of twenty looking for casual work at the lodge. He had very little experience and just his own Ovambo language Oshiwombo.The manager at the time liked his attitude and decided to give him a chance even though he had to disappoint people almost weekly who called looking for work. Over ten years Mika worked his way from casual gardening work to maintenance work before moving inside to help in the office and in the dining room. He learned quickly and began picking up some English, Afrikaans and German from guests. He gained more and more responsibilities and became a very capable guide often leading tours of the farm and the cave. Mika developed a reputation as a hard working conscientious worker with a very pleasant manner. He learned quickly and sharpened his computer and office skills over a period of time becoming quite proficient. When the previous manager decided to leave Ghaub suddenly four years ago the company appointed Mika temporary manager which was quite a promotion considering his age and lack of experience. It was a thankless role as he received little support from the company who were pulling away from Ghaub and trying to sell the property. Against such a difficult backdrop Mika did an amazing job and almost single handily kept the lodge running to a high standard to the best of his ability. When we arrived here in August 2007 Mika was then filling several roles and was a courteous host and extremely warm in his welcome. It was he who told me originally that the lodge was for sale when I remarked that this place was so beautiful that I could easily stay here. Mika is now proficient in English, Afrikaans and most impressively his German is excellent which is invaluable as we have so many German guests. He is proficient dealing with tour operators, confirming bookings and sending out invoices. He was doing most of the banking and stock taking exceptionally well and I have learned at least as much from him as I have been able to pass on in return. He is proud of his roots and origins and is an example to all young Ovambo men what they can achieve if they are prepared to work hard. I trust Mika implicitly and can safely say that he is the most vital member of the Ghaub team. In fact the whole operation could not manage without him and we hope that he will be with us for a long time.

Christofine Dei Geis

Christofine is a Damara lady who is our senior cook and has been a member of the Ghaub team for eight years. Herself and Mika have two children together -Nelson who is six years and Doreen who is four years old. Christofine is a good chef and goes about her work diligently. When we are quiet with guests she also helps the girls in the laundry. Damara people have a very distinct language full of clicks and unusual sounds. It is very interesting to listen to two Damara people having a conversation. It is not unusual here for children to stay with their grandparents so that they can go to school in town while their parents work away from home. Chistofine's children usually visit for school holidays and it is a routine to collect all the children once the holidays begin in Tsumeb around sixty kilometres away. Christofine and Mika are no longer together as Mika has married an Ovambo lady and they now also have two children Reuben and Marian. There is a quiet determination about Christofine and she would be opinionated but I have always found her to be reliable, punctual and hard working. In fact I like her spirit and encourage her to be assertive and stand up for what she believes to be right. Too many young local people here are inclined to bow down to authority and accept that they are somehow less entitled. I like to encourage the staff to believe in themselves and insist on been treated with dignity and respect. at all times.

Martin Shinyala

Martin works outside in the garden and looks after general maintenance work around the lodge. He is also here for about eight years and goes about his work quietly. He has very little English so communication can be difficult. He really only speaks Oshiwombo which sounds like Japanese to me. Martin has a partner Ndili and one daughter Monica who usually travels with us on the school run. Martin's brother Lucas works at the Engen garage in Tsumeb and I find him to be friendly and amiable. They are almost identical even though there is two years between them. I received an invitation to Lucas' wedding during the year which promised to be quite a novel experience but had to decline as it clashed with one of my visits home to Ireland. Sometimes I think Martin is a bit shy and reserved but it's really due to the difficulty with the language and his ability to communicate. His duties also include milking the cows and cutting the grass around the lodge which is now much easier since we bought our new John Deere tractor mower. Martin is quite a good footballer and enjoys our occasional soccer matches and makes a decent left back.

Immanuel Muteto

Immanuel or Tato as we call him for short is an incredibly interesting character. He is Kavango which is a different tribe from the North East of the country towards the Caprivi. Tato is aged thirty eight and has a real good heart. He is so obliging even though like Martin his English is limited. When you address him he always answers 'excuse' while struggling to understand the question. He is incredibly strong and talented with his hands. He can fix anything mechanical and would make a great handyman on any farm in Ireland. Tato is also very family conscious and I notice him sending money home to his family whenever he can and also looking out for his nieces and nephews. The Kavango people are generally hard working in my experience and I find them easy to get along with. Tato is popular with all the staff and seems to have assumed the role of spokesman for the group. Whenever anyone is in trouble they seem to look to Tato for direction. He is always the first to speak up if there is a perceived injustice but always in a respectful way. I notice too that Tato has been given to job of dividing out the tips from the gratuity box left at reception. He takes great care and every cent is accounted for. I would love to bring him to Ireland for a holiday but he has never travelled far and heads home to his family as soon as he gets a break from the lodge.

Lotto Haufiku

Lotto is one of the younger lads and joined the staff about three years ago. In the beginning I wasn't sure what to make of him as he was distant and unfriendly when approached. I had to encourage him to smile and it became an in house joke as the staff started to tease him by saying glimlag Lotto which is Afrikaans for smile! Then I realised that he was also quite shy and avoided contact when he could. I now know him much better and consider him one of the most reliable members of the team. His English is also poor but he is trying his best to learn more from the girls. He is also Oshiwombo but is popular too with everyone and is always willing to help out. His duties are mostly outside in the garden and general maintenance but he will always help the girls in the rooms or help with the washing up when the lodge is busy. More recently he has taken over the main responsibility for looking after the horses and he is a capable rider. He exercises the horses three times weekly and brings guests out to view the farm on horseback. Lotto is also the best car washer we have and he takes great pride in polishing up the lodge vehicles at least once a week.

Ida Dei-Geis

Ida joined Ghaub three years ago and is a younger sister of Christofine. The family live in Tsumeb and I am still meeting more members of the family after twelve months here. Ida is our senior lady in the laundry and is also largely responsible for preparing the rooms for the guests. I must say that Ida is the most Irish of all the staff and has a wicked sense of humour. I find her to be very considerate and moderate in her views. If there is a problem I will seek her out to get to the bottom of whatever is going on as I know she will give a fair and measured account of what's happening. Damara women are proud and very loyal to their families. Ida has perhaps the best English of all the staff after Mika and has a sharp and willing mind. We are lucky to have her and I fear sometimes that she will leave us for better things. Whenever I need a pickup I can usually rely on Ida to lift the mood with her jokes. Despite my attempts to encourage her to stretch herself and work inside she has declined to work as a waitress out of shyness mostly although I think she would be good in that area and appreciated by the guests. Also Ida and Lotto are a couple and had a daughter together recently which they named Antoinette after my son Anthony who was a good friend to both them when he was here.

Frieda Gawas

I call Frieda and Ida the terrible twins sometimes as they are rarely apart and the best of friends. First cousins I think although it's hard to understand just exactly what the family connections are sometimes. Frieda is also very popular and full of fun. She has a terrific singing voice and I will often hear her singing aloud in her own language as she goes about her work. Frieda lost her daughter of three years earlier in the year which was a terrible tragedy. Always smiling and in good form Frieda never complains and accepts everything as God's plan. She has a great attitude to life and works really hard as well. At one stage she had a boyfriend who used to arrive out at the lodge on a small motor-bike from Grootfontein. I used to tease her a little and called him Pizza man as he reminded me of the guys at home in Dublin who go around delivery Pizzas on old Honda 50s. Frieda heard he was cheating on her after several months together and when I asked her how she was doing she replied "I am fine Mr Gerry, I will just have to find another Pizza man!

Johanna Frans

Johanna is one of the newer members of the Ghaub staff who I found in Tsumeb last year when I needed a chef urgently when my previous second cook Martha left us suddenly. I interviewed Johanna and thought she could be trusted and she seemed to have reasonable cooking experience. I promised her a three month contract at first and a fulltime job if she proved to be up to it. She is also Oshiwombo which is an advantage although to be fair we have never had any clashes between the tribes. Some lodges refuse to mix the cultures for fear of problems among the different traditions. Johanna needed time to adjust and seemed at first to have two speeds both of which were slow but I liked her and thought she would fit in eventually. About four moths after she arrived it became obvious that she was expecting a baby and I suppose out of desperation for a job she held back on telling us that she was already pregnant when she joined us. But overall she has done a good job and gets on well with the others which is crucial.

Andreas Likuwa

Andreas is another interesting member of the team and I have to admit I am particularly pleased that he is doing so well. I needed a barman/waiter last year when Erenst walked out and decided to hold interviews as I had a growing number of CVS on my desk. Whenever I get asked for work in town I usually suggest that the person sends me their CV and I will consider them the next time there is a vacancy. To cut a long story short eight people turned up at the lodge one Tuesday that I set aside for interviews for a new position. Andreas was probably the least experienced of them all and had very little to recommend him. But I warmed to him and I decided to give him a chance because of his manner and attitude. For the first month he dropped everything and made countless mistakes taking the wrong orders to the wrong tables and becoming flustered in front of guests. I had to have a chat with him but he responded really well and I am chuffed that he is now a very capable and pleasant waiter and good barman. He keeps the dining room spotless and always has a ready smile for the visitors. Andreas is Kavango like Tato which was one of the reason I took a chance with him. He is quiet, unassuming and popular with all the other staff who recognise his good intent even when he makes mistakes. Andreas is also a useful footballer and really comes out of his shell on the soccer field and expresses himself really well. I hope he stays with us for a long time.

Klaus Ndjamba

Klaus is another interesting character who joined the team in December. He was recommended to us by Andre as he had worked at Andre's farm near Okanhandja and Andre was of the opinion that he would be an asset to us at the lodge. A very personable young man just twenty one years old Klaus is what's called a Nama Damara. Obviously his first name suggests a German connection as it is quite unusual for a young Namibian black man. Apparently his Grandmother gave him the name Klaus as she was close to a neighbouring German family many years ago. Klaus was immediately well accepted by everyone and is a skilled personable young man. He is very good with languages and a capable driver and guide. He quickly was given some duties that relieved Mika substantially and gives him more time in the office and dealing with operators and guests. Klaus is very adaptable and fits in wherever needed including helping out in the dining room as a waiter and barman. He has a deep rich singing voice and we have started to introduce a bit of local culture to the guests with Klaus's help of late. Sometimes when we have a large booking the staff will entertain the guests after dinner with some traditional songs and dance. It is just another feature which guests enjoy and the staff also enjoys entertaining. Klaus is also good with the horses and helps Lotto to keep them exercised. Klaus could go places and I imagine he may eventually move on to bigger and better things. He deserves the opportunity but I am pleased to have him for now. He is pleasant, courteous and very respectful and a good team player.

Hilma Kangili Mbuale

Hilma is the baby of the family and our newest recruit. She is the only Herero member and I found her out of necessity when Johanna was suddenly rushed to hospital in January. We needed another cook immediately and I was at a loss before deciding to contact the catering college on Oshikati which is around three hundred kilometres away. Perhaps it was luck but they told me they had a promising young recruit who might fit the bill and agreed to release her for a month on trial. That was on a Monday and the following Friday I met the bus from Oshakati at the head of the road as it passed on its way to Windhoek on an extremely wild wet night which made driving hazardous. I will never forget it as the gravel road was like an ice rink and with the driving rain visibility was extremely poor. Hilma arrived on time however and we made it back to the lodge in one piece. Hilma has fitted in well and we offered her a full time contract after she proved herself although at first I wasn't convinced. Her experience was negligible but she has learned quickly and has a great attitude. Herero are also proud people whose history is remarkable for the suffering they experienced as they were driven off their lands by the Germans many years ago. Known for their colourful dresses and fancy headgear they can be spotted in most of the bigger towns especially Swakopmund and Omaruru. Hilma is learning quickly and we now have a good united hardworking team.

12

WELCOME BACK TO CIVILIZATION

I still marvel each morning when I pull back the curtains as the sun is coming up across the horizon. My window faces due east and within ten minutes the sky changes from navy blue to a pale yellow and then a deep orange just before the sun appears. It is quite a sight and for me it's the best time of the day. It's easy to hop out of bed at that hour when you witness such a spectacular daily event. This is my time and I usually have finished feeding the animals before the staff come in to prepare breakfast for the guests. The wall of sound hits you first as you emerge from the room. It's mostly birds and insects but always some unidentifiable sounds as well. Sometimes there will be young deer, some warthogs or a few monkeys searching for an early breakfast as you pass through the garden. Once the dog, the cats, the chickens and the horses are fed in that order then it's the turn of the Eland who is fast becoming the star attraction around the lodge. Now twelve weeks old he rambles around the grounds during the day and arrives at the back door bang on 4.00pm for his bottle of milk before we put him back in for the night. He is quite tame now and the guests often take turns to feed him. Then shortly after 7.00am it's time to prepare breakfast and I am busy setting up the buffet which offers guests several options including a local or a continental breakfast. I do a little cooking but I mostly look after the rashers for the bacon and eggs which are popular. After tidying up it's down to office work for a couple of hours as you can be busy with tour operators, calls, marketing and planning new ways to bring in more business.

December was busier for a number of reasons. We decided to offer a special deal to Namibians to make it more affordable for locals to stay at the farm. Most lodges tend to operate European prices that may not seem very expensive in Europe but are impossible for the locals here. We decided to offer our rooms at N$500.00 or 50 Euro per night including dinner, bed and breakfast based on a two night stay. We advertised in two of the daily newspapers and received a good immediate response. It meant that we had a busy Christmas and now people are coming out from Tsumeb and Grootfontein for week-ends and sometimes for a day visit to the cave or to go for long walks through the farm. This reminds me of an awkward situation I had to deal with earlier in the year when we had callers on several Sundays who arrived with picnic baskets and car loads of kids with the intention of having a barbecue on our lawn by the pool. They were quite shocked and upset when I explained that we do not allow that anymore as this was a private hotel for guests only. Apparently they had been coming for years camping out on the grass and often leaving a mess before heading home without spending a Dollar for the privilege. I am convinced that it is a power struggle as the local white people were taking advantage of the locally managed lodge and pushing their luck. No more however and even though I received bad press at first we no longer have any unreasonable day visitors expecting the impossible.

December 1st was significant for the fact that the farm manager Billy decided to begin the planting of the maize a full seven weeks ahead of last year. He predicted that the rains would be earlier this year and he seems to have been correct again! The planting is fascinating to watch for the uninformed farmer like me and although slow by Irish standards it is effective and carefully planned. Timing is crucial without irrigation pivots and so much depends on getting the seed into the ground at the right time. It takes about two weeks to complete the planting and you can see the difference in the areas that were planted first after just three weeks. Now after eight weeks the maize is flush, green and healthy looking as a result of the combination of isolated heavy showers and warm sunshine.

Around this time we added mosquito nets to the rooms to make the rooms more comfortable for guests. They are purely for decoration as we are fortunate not to have to worry about mosquitoes in this area. I paid N$4,000 for nets for ten twin rooms covering both beds. I think it was a bargain although we had to put them up ourselves. I also began to notice around this time that I was losing weight rapidly and I just may have discovered the secret to diet and weight control. Forget your Atkins diet and your neutron (remember that was all the rage a few years ago).That was the one that gave you a list of foods to avoid including bread, alcohol and sweet things! You spend lots of money, have a blood test done and you are given a list of foods to take moderately and ones to stay clear of. An old friend tried it once and on his list of foods to avoid were aubergines. He never heard of them! I used to tease him about missing his aubergines whenever I met him. Anyway forget about exercise, going to the gym, drinking more water counting calories and getting more sleep. Just eat less!! Guaranteed to work.

Had an incredible experience recently which I should share. It's a story about an Aardvark which is a first cousin of an ant-eater. In mid December we had a very nice young German couple stay with us for two nights. It was their second visit to Namibia and they had travelled most of the country. Their main interest was the wildlife and they had some brilliant photos of different animals in their own habitat. They approached me after dinner on their last night requesting a big favour. They pleaded with me to take them on a late night drive around the farm as a last chance to spot the elusive Aardvark which was the only animal they had not spotted during two trips and hours of searching. Could I help? Well I told them that I had only ever seen one Aardvark during the past twelve months which was by chance as I was driving the staff home after dinner one night. This large creature ambled out the gate in front of us caught in the lights of the car. As they are notoriously shy animals it was a rare but fortunate sighting. Despite doing my best to put the visitors off the idea they insisted that we try and were happy to pay for the inconvenience. So we set off shortly after 10.00pm when all the other guests had retired for the night and inched our way towards the foot of the mountains in our old trusty game viewing vehicle. I was hoping we might see a few Kudu at least but the chances of even that were slim. I tried to build a bit of atmosphere after 20 minutes without as much as a pair of eyes peering from the trees and so suggested we stop and walk to a clearing one hundred yards up the path. Armed with flashlights we walked slowly listening out for anything out of the ordinary. In hindsight it was foolish as you never know what's lurking in the shadows here. After a short walk we stopped, turned off the torches and waited in silence. Not thirty seconds later we heard movement to our left in the bushes and the guy who was especially enthusiastic directed his torch and focused on a large Aardvark scurrying through the bush. You couldn't make it up! It may have been only a brief sighting but the guests were delighted and convinced that I was stringing them along and was really an ace tracker of rare animals. Little did they know that it was a million to one chance but you just never know here. Later we spotted some giant toads at one of the water hole that were making quite a racket. There was also a sighting of a large pack of guinea fowl settling down for the night in the branches of an overhanging Marulu tree before we headed back. More satisfied customers and a relieved guide just about getting away with it!

The week before I headed home for Christmas I brought the staff to Swakopmund as promised. Now a trip to the seaside is nothing out of the ordinary for most people but when you consider that these were seven young adults who were living in a Country with a coastline that stretches for hundreds of miles and had never before seen the sea in their lives then it was something special. I could not get over the fact that none of them had ever seen seawater. If Namibia was a land locked country you could perhaps understand that it could be possible as travel is difficult. But it was different here as it has more to do with the fact that the local people don't go on holiday as we understand it. When the staff get their annual leave they always return home to their families typically and end up working flat out to improve small plots of land or contribute in any way they can to boost the family income. They often come back to work tired but that's how it works and they wouldn't have it any differently. You can only imagine the level of excitement as we packed the cars for the five hour journey to the coast. The landscape changes dramatically as you head west which was a wonder in itself to most of the passengers. A short stop in Karibib around half way for cool drinks and our packed sandwiches and then quickly we are back on the road for another two hundred kilometres on good tar surfaces with little traffic. I have travelled to Swakopmund a few times and the countryside reminds me of Colorado even though I have never been there. It is mostly semi-desert surrounded on all sides by distant mountains and looks like a scene from an old Clint Eastwood western. We arrived late afternoon and headed straight to the beach. It would be impossible to describe the reaction from the backseat when the sea came into view for the first time. It was a mixture of wonder, awe and excitement. Andreas just kept saying Wow over and over. As soon as we pulled up Lotto was first out and did an acrobatic somersault dive into the water fully clothed and was lucky not to injure himself as it was quite shallow. Despite the cold Atlantic water he came up smiling. I took some photos but they really do not capture the moment. It was very special and will live with me forever. The whole week-end was a success despite very basic accommodation in the municipality bungalows. It reminded me of a Butlins camp in the nineteen seventy's but the staff were delighted with it. I had to kick up a fuss to get a kettle, some cutlery and a few pots and pans from reception as the rooms were so basic and without essentials. On the Saturday we drove to Cape Cross which is about one hundred Kilometres north along the Skeleton coastline to visit the seal colony and there must have been twenty thousand seals in a relatively small area. Later we were invited for a barbecue at the home of the previous manager at Ghaub. I had never met him before but was anxious to visit as he really deserves most of the credit for the way the lodge looks today. He is a German, Mr Volker Steinstrater and he managed the lodge for six years under the previous owners Oldhaver and List. Volker is obviously an extremely skilled craftsman as there are many examples of his creativity evident around the lodge to this day. He put in the swimming pool, the hide where guests can view animals at the nearby waterhole and the distinctive bar counter made from Tamboti wood. He and his wife made the staff feel very welcome as most of them were at the lodge during his time. There was an interesting dynamic which I noticed as the staff never quite relaxed and seemed a little uneasy throughout the evening despite the warm welcome from our hosts. I think it had something to do with meeting their former boss in a different setting and struggling to feel comfortable in such an informal relaxed manner. Mr Steinstrater told me in confidence that his heart is still in Ghaub and that he and his wife both had huge regrets about leaving the lodge.

We headed back early on Sunday morning and the good mood continued all the way home. Everyone individually thanked me after and said how much it meant to them. It has been good for morale even though morale has never been a problem here. They will certainly remember their first trip to the sea

On December 18th I went home for Christmas and I was really looking forward to a break and to seeing the family. It had seemed like such a long time and I was wondering about the future. The business was definitely showing signs of improvement much to my relief. The lodge was busier and the farm was in good shape after a strong harvest and a good calving season. But even though that was gratifying I was having doubts about coming back. The good times were fantastic but there were also tough and challenging moments. Overall I was feeling incredibly isolated and cut off from the family. I would have lots to ponder over Christmas and lots to discuss with Marian, my rock. Stopping off overnight in Windhoek I again had an interesting day in the city. Such a mix of colour and always the odd surprise. This time I noticed the Himba ladies selling their handmade crafts on the lawn in front of the Post Office off Independence Avenue. Covered in red clay from head to toe and with just a loin cloth covering their modesty they seem out of place in a bustling modern city. I was now very familiar with Windhoek airport and passed through without a problem quickly. I actually got bumped up to business class thanks to my cousin Martin who was travelling to London to fly the plane back. Apparently the same pilot cannot fly such a long route on consecutive days by International aviation law. I wasn't complaining and took advantage of the comfort and special attention. Sometimes you can get an upgrade for as little as one hundred pounds sterling. I would recommend it if travelling for a short holiday as a ten hour flight can be uncomfortable with little leg room. I actually sat for a while with a friendly English tour operator who was visiting Namibia for the first time in the hope of introducing more English tourists to the delights of this unique place. We hit it off extremely well and have remained in touch.

Christmas was brilliant at home and I decided quickly that I would return until Easter only. I will most likely return to my old job at the Rutland. It will be a bit of a culture shock but I will be ready. I will keep in contact with the lodge from home and hopefully appoint another manager to assist Mika. Hopefully when the lads are older we will be in a position to consider moving to Namibia permanently. I have experienced enough over the past year to convince me that we could make a future here.

During the holidays I made a late decision to book a night out with Marian and her sister Colette who was home for a short visit from Canada. I was looking for a good gig as we all enjoy live music but there wasn't a lot to choose from. Reading the Evening Herald I noticed an add for The Last Waltz Tribute show in Whelan's of Wexford Street. For some reason I had missed The Last Waltz first time round and only had a vague notion that it was a farewell concert of sorts from a group called The Band who were big in the sixties. The ad mentioned that they would be joined by sound-alike's Eric Clapton, Bob Dylan, Neil Young, Neil Diamond and Van Morrison among others on stage! Now as a late convert to Van Morrison and a life long fan of Bob Dylan and Eric Clapton I thought it might be worth a shout and booked three tickets over the phone without any great expectations. Turned out to be a fantastic night which introduced me to a genre that had passed me by for some reason much to my regret. I loved every minute of it as the music was excellent with a really tight talented band. I got a tap on the shoulder during the first half from an old friend Larry O Loughlin who knew I had been in Africa and was surprised to see me. The music was so loud we could hardly hear each other so we agreed to meet up for a chat later. Then out of the blue during the second half the same Larry arrives out on stage much to my surprise in the guise of Bobby Charles singing "Down South in New Orleans"! I had no idea he could sing and was blown away by his performance which added to a memorable night. I have since become a convert and a true fan of The Band and can't understand why we don't hear more of their music. Such talented musicians and song writers they deserve to be included up there with the all time greats. I also have kept in touch with The Group aka The Band who consist of three Butler Brothers and friends from Dublin, whose Dad Pierce did a tribute act to Neil Diamond for years around the Country and still performs in the show. If you enjoy really good live music give them a try!

I also decided to travel to Tullamore in the midlands to check out how the Offaly footballers were shaping up for the season ahead and to meet up with some old friends. The O Byrne cup in a cold O' Connor Park in early January in Ireland is about as far away from Namibia as you can get. The company was great even if the match wasn't and we retired afterwards to the Bridge House for tea and scones like the old days. We received a warm welcome from Noel, the manager who had always looked after us well after matches in the past. We had a good catch up and the lads were very interested in how life in Africa was. There and then they decided to visit in February and as it stands I am expecting a gang of five Biffos to arrive on Feb 25th which should be some crack. I plan to put an interesting itinerary together for them and take them to the lodge for a few days. I am particularly looking forward to taking them to the Sunday service at the Maria Bronn School. I kept in touch with Mika regularly from home and the staff did a great job in my absence. It was easier coming back this time as I was pretty sure it would be my last stint for a while and I was planning to be extremely busy over the next three months.

Mika took his well earned break upon my return and went home to visit his family in Ovamboland. He bought his first ever car over Christmas, an open backed small Toyota which he is very proud of. He looks after it so well and for some reason he reminds me of Postman Pat when I see him coming up the road. I really miss him when he is not here as he is so reliable and hard working. For the past three weeks I have had long days as we have guests who like to have breakfast at 6.45am each morning and we have to start an hour before that in order to have everything ready. We currently have three long term guests from the new cement factory which is been built in Otavi nearby. Two German gentlemen and an Argentinean approached us before Christmas looking for rooms for ten weeks on a full board basis. After a bit of haggling we agreed on an all inclusive price which was acceptable to all. It was good business for the lodge as it meant 30% occupancy for at least ten weeks and perhaps longer before we sold another room. They are ideal guests as they are gone at 7.30am each morning and return at 7.30pm for dinner and then retire early to bed. One of the party followed us to the Maria Bronn for church on their second Sunday and I noticed he was driving a bit erratically. The following day Billy, the farm manager, mentioned to me that he was nearly run off the road by one of our guests that previous morning. The staff had also commented about the speed he was driving past their homes in the evening. I shouldn't have been surprised when two days later he hit a Kudu around ten kilometres down the gravel road and was lucky to survive. What surprised me most was his reaction as he didn't appear too bothered explaining that it was only a rental and he was well insured. The car was a complete right off and the garage man who came to collect the car said in all his years in the game he had never seen a car so badly damaged without a fatality. Although there was relief all round this for me was an example of why car insurance is so expensive here. You read about regular accidents on gravel roads especially with tourists involved driving recklessly in their 4x 4s thinking they are competing in The Paris Dakker rally! Be careful if you are travelling here especially after dark as there are often animals on the road. Our Argentinean visitor is another intriguing character. After a bad start when he seemed to complain about the tiniest matter we now get on famously. He is fond of his food and is another who seems to think that a buffet is a challenge to eat as much as you can at one sitting.

Whenever I am home friends often ask about local customs and trends here. I do find it fascinating to see how people relate to each other and how Namibians and Afrikaners interact. It is interesting to watch how parents discipline their children sometimes. I noticed on one occasion when a young White African couple with young children were staying with us and were quite heavy handed whenever the children misbehaved. You can see children getting smacked in public which seems to be acceptable here. There was another interesting occurrence recently at one of our weekly meetings with the staff which we generally hold outside. During the discussion of a serious issue there was a sudden general burst of laughter and I was at a complete loss as to what it was all about. I usually lead the meeting in English and Mika translates in Afrikaans for the staff. When I asked them to explain what was said that was so funny they all piped in that it was a particular cry from a bird in the garden that I had hardly noticed that was making a racket. Seemingly when this bird cries out in such a fashion it means that someone is pregnant and as the staff recognised the familiar call at once they exploded into fits of laughter and speculated who would be having an addition to their family next! I also had an interesting encounter recently with another policeman at a roadblock on the way in to Grootfontein. During the holiday season the police erect roadblocks on the approaches and exits to all the bigger towns. It is part security and part road safety as they remind people about driving carefully. Usually they are friendly and wave you through but I always feel just a little uneasy when asked to stop because you can never be absolutely sure. On this occasion the guy asked me for my licence and had a few questions about where I worked and where I was from. I was polite as usual and trying to be friendly when he seemed to change his tune and aggressively questioned my status here as if I was working illegally. Even though I knew I was legit it was unnerving as you just never know with these guys. Once he seemed satisfied with my answers he changed his tune again completely and offered to buy the buggy I was driving. He was quite serious and seemed to know that it might be for sale. I took his number and promised to call him soon before he waved us on. It was another one of those encounters that would just never happen at home.

We have been busy during the month of January compared to this time last year. Then I remember having several nights without guests but this year we have had guests every day. We had some interesting guests to stay recently including an American couple who live with their two young children in Botswana. Also we had a young couple from South Africa who were on their way to Botswana to run a new lodge and had everything they possess with them as they were moving lock, stock and barrel to begin a new life in another country leaving their families behind. There has been a noticeable rise in the temperatures of late and the heat is just about bearable at times. We actually were praying for rain which I never thought I would welcome but it certainly was a pleasant relief when the heavens opened and that familiar smell filled the air once again. It is hard to describe but magical and refreshing.

I turned fifty last week and it was all a bit strange passing that milestone out in the back of beyond with nobody to share it with. I thought it would just pass like any other day until the staff surprised me with a cake at 7.00am when I arrived down to breakfast. I was in for a bigger shock when I struggled to cut through the cake which they had prepared to discover that it was in fact a lump of dry cow dung covered in chocolate! Just another local joke for occasions like this and there was nervous laughter at first as they checked out whether or not I saw the funny side of it. Otherwise it was another typical day and the work went on. A few calls from home later were welcome but overall it was a bit of an anti-climax. I will always remember however where I spent my 50th birthday though which would have seemed totally out of the question a few short years ago. I notice too that lately my language is gone to the dogs. I was always uncomfortable about swearing. It just never came natural to me for some reason. I wouldn't be at all prudish or object to others ffing and blinding but for me it just didn't feel right. But lately I seem to have tapped into a flow of self expression that would shock a docker! There are days when I am seething with unreasonable guests and although on the outside it's all sweetness and smiles, inside it's f *%@ this and b**&%## to that. Maybe it's old age!

I picked up a few DVDs at the airport on the way back last time. Really enjoyed the Film "Once" with Glen Hansard. Haven't enjoyed a film as much in ages and it was all made for less than 100,000 Euro. It reminded me in ways of another old favourite of mine. Probably my favourite film of all time called 'Truly, Madly Deeply'. Check it out. For a laugh I also brought back a copy of the Sound of Music and gave it to the Sisters at the Maria Bronn School. When I went back the following Sunday they were all chatting about it. Can you picture a group of black Namibian nuns crowding round a small screen watching Julie Andrews for the first time?

The internet keeps me up to date with the Premiership in England and the Gaa news from home. Sport has been such a part of my life always and I always have an interest when there is Irish involvement. Anything from golf to cricket I will watch and have spent hours watching sport on T V. over many years. It would be interesting to work out how many hours in total. Over here has given me a different perspective and perhaps now I am feeling those hours could have been put to better use. I intend to be more selective whenever I return back to the first world. Or maybe Andre was right when he greeted me once on my return to Namibia with the words-"Welcome back to civilisation". Maybe this is in fact more civilised here and this is where you find real quality of life.

13

IF YOU BURN A HOUSE YOU CANNOT CONSEAL THE SMOKE!

There was a definite feeling of time running out for me here as February arrived and passed in a flash. Mika had been on holiday for three weeks in January and returned on the 31st and I was so relieved to have him back. I didn't have a day off for the three weeks so when I returned from the Maria Bronn service on Sunday February 1st I decided I would go for a long hike around the farm and head for the hills. It was particularly warm and humid as I set off and fortunately I brought along some water and a packed lunch as I will explain shortly. Bono came along as well as he rarely leaves my side. I had planned to take a four hour walk through the hills and hopefully see some animals and parts of the farm that I hadn't previously explored. It was to turn into an eventful day.

I headed off shortly before 1.00pm and for an hour the land was familiar and a part of the farm I knew well. The sun was extremely hot but there was a soft breeze blowing and I was enjoying the exercise and the views. I spotted lots of animals as they didn't hear me coming on foot and was feeling very content with myself before I took a break after an hour on an overhanging rock half way up the first mountain. The view was breathtaking and I was overcome by a deep sense of calmness I have rarely felt. Bono was beginning to wish he stayed at home as he lay panting in the shade under a large fruit tree. Anyway I decided to push on after a short break over the crest to a flatter area between two mountains and my mind was racing for some reason. I had this strange feeling of peacefulness and my head was full of creative thoughts. I could only guess that the surroundings were allowing me to access something within which is usually beyond reach. It got me into thinking that perhaps most of us don't tap into our potential as we are too busy in our heads. All of a sudden I could remember poems and long passages from texts going back to my schooldays and it was really strange for a time. Irish seemed easy and I could recall lots of French words I had long since forgotten. I remembered a poem by Milton on his blindness and the line "He also serves who only stands and waits" (He certainly wasn't referring to corner forwards!).My head remained full of jokes and amusing anecdotes and I regretted not having brought a pencil to make some notes.

After another hour walking I decided to climb what looked like a small hill which I thought should bring me back in the direction of the lodge. As I climbed the undergrowth became thicker and the path began to disappear. I couldn't see up or down and had to decide quickly to push on or turn back. "Two roads diverged in a yellow wood and I took the one less travelled by and that has made all the difference."! Where did that come from? I chose discretion and spent twenty minutes walking round in circles struggling to find the way out. Just as I was beginning to panic I found a path that looked familiar and luckily recognised the direction I was heading. Just as I reached the clearing I nearly stepped on a chameleon that must have been three foot long. I didn't even know they had chameleons here and this thing flashed his forked tongue at me and didn't look a bit pleased to have his afternoon snooze disrupted. I discovered later that they are quite harmless. A few minutes later a huge turtle was wandering down the path towards me and withdrew into his shell as I passed.

The rest of the journey was relatively uneventful although I regained that sense of inner peace and contentment. When I returned to the lodge Mika told me that if I had kept going instead of turning round I would never have made it as there is a higher crest beyond the one I was climbing that you can't see from the other side. I could easily have been out all night and in genuine danger. Sometimes it pays to accept your limitations. All this and it was still only February 1st. For some reason this day remains with me vividly imprinted in my mind.

The beginning of the month was busy with guests and I noticed we had some interesting visitors. There was an English guy named Greg who I met by chance a few weeks previously in Tsumeb as we were both paying our phone bills in Telecom. Whenever I hear an English accent I usually stop to chat and Greg told me he was from Grimsby originally but now living in Namibia for the past eighteen months. All I know about Grimsby is that like Kinvara in the West of Ireland it is considered a drinking town with a fishing problem. Greg was friendly and promised to visit the lodge with his Namibian girlfriend soon. Sure enough he arrived out having made a booking with Mika. I thought he was German as Mika had misspelled his name and was surprised when he arrived. His girlfriend was a Naomi Campbell lookalike while Greg has been married twice previously and must be in his fifties. They have been together seven months and plan to settle down soon. It was an interesting evening as Greg chatted non stop while Naomi just sat in silence staring at him lovingly. I suppose one shouldn't judge but for me they seemed an unlikely match and an example of something I have noticed here with local young women with older European partners and it all seems a little desperate. There was another example of what I thought initially looked like an unlikely couple I met at the internet café in Grootfontein. Owned seemingly by an attractive white lady and her partner, a brute of a man who could pass for an unsuccessful boxer. I just thought it was strange until one day the phone rang and the lady picked up and spent the next fifteen minutes chatting loudly to one of her friends in Afrikaans. She had a cackling laugh like a witch and I eventually had to get out of there. Maybe there is a price for living with beauty after all!

We have a running joke here with the staff that whenever they return from holiday I pretend that I can't remember their name as they have been away so long. They take it very seriously and are genuinely put out that they might be forgotten and take great pains to remind me. Their customs still amuse me hugely. For example when they greet each other in the morning it lasts for several seconds and there are several exchanges of greeting before they go about their work. It can go something like Hello, How are you, mmm, how is it ,mmm, how's it going, mmm, everything alright, mmm, even if you know the person well and you see them every day. I have also noticed recently when you pass a group of road workers or the equivalent of the county council working away on some road scheme there will be several women in the troop digging away and mucking in with the guys. Clearly the Namibian corporation is an equal opportunities destroyer. Also I have always tried not to upset anyone here by being rude. There are so many different groups of black people that it's hard to know where they are from of what group they belong. But apparently it's quite alright to ask them what tribe they belong to. This is not an offensive question and is generally welcomed as the people like to share their origin and their background.

Around the second week in February I drove to Windhoek to pick up our new car. It's actually a two year old Toyota Hilux diesel 3.0 Double cab which is ideal for local conditions and suits our needs ideally. It's really a beautiful car and it will turn out to be much cheaper to run than the old twenty year old Toyota Raider that we have been using which was written off at least once! I was actually caught speeding in the old car coming through Otavi on the way down to Windhoek. I was in another world daydreaming when a car flashed me as I approached the town. I thought to myself who was that as I didn't recognise the car and realised too late that they were trying to send me the familiar warning sign that there were speedies ahead or speed control cops. They clocked me at seventy five Kilometres in a sixty zone and made an issue of taking me from the car and showing me clearly on their speed gun that I was well past the limit. I chanced my arm not for the first time and stated that I was shocked that the old car was capable of doing seventy five and I was actually on the way to trade it in. The guy either took pity on me or couldn't understand my thick Irish accent but he let me off with a warning this time and I didn't even have to offer him a bribe!

With the new car you have to be careful on gravel roads though. After rain the roads get very slippery and although I usually drive carefully it's like driving on ice sometimes. Only a few days after getting it I had a skid on the way to Grootfontein and I knew if I over corrected too quickly I could have turned the car over. So another lesson learned. Can you imagine crashing a new car after three days! I would not have been able to show my face. When I was down in Windhoek I picked up the new signs we had ordered for the lodge. When I arrived here last year all the signs approaching the lodge on the tar and gravel roads were old, rusty and falling apart. I took them down and scraped off the old paintwork before rewriting the name Guest Farm Ghaub in bold capitals. But in truth it was very amateurish and it was time to get a more professional job done. I spoke to our old friend Alan Hendry, the Scotsman living in Windhoek and between us we designed new signs using the new company logo. We agreed a price of N\$11,000 for eight large signs which are almost 70cms x 40cms. When erecting signs on the public roads here you have to consider a number of important issues. Firstly they must be termite proof as ants and other insects will make short work of anything that is not durable. Secondly they also have to be weather proof as the heavy rains during the wet season will destroy anything flimsy so a hard metal is a must. Finally they have to be human proof because if they are not secured to the ground and welded tight to supports someone will run off with them. It was a reasonable price and the end result was very professional and they look really well as you approach the lodge. Had another interesting experience when I was down in Windhoek. While having a quiet meal alone in the hotel a group of four locals, two men and two women came in for dinner and sat close by. When the waiter called at their table with menus they loudly declared that they couldn't read and asked him to recommend anything as long as there was meat in it. Another example of the importance of meat and the lack of embarrassment in front of strangers. Meat is so important here and the local people believe that a meal is not a proper meal unless it contains plenty of meat. I see people buying meat in a butcher type shop in Tsumeb and they get little bags of bones or small cuts of sausage like meat as you would buy a packet of sweets at home. It almost seems like a badge of honour to wear as if they are saying "Look at me I can afford to buy meat."

Still listening to lots of Irish music on long journeys especially. Can you remember The Lookalikes, The Stunning, Cry before Dawn, Those Nervous Animals and The Blades. I used to love these bands years ago and their music is still good today. Not much time for leisure although I did have one game of golf not long ago. I played with a local black guy who works at the local Cash and Carry shop. I met him a few times and he was always asking for a game. He was well able to play off a handicap of about four and had a good natural swing. The course in Tsumeb is like a reasonably good public course at home with good greens. We avoided the rain and had the place to ourselves. It seems that people only play golf here on Wednesdays and Saturdays. I was a bit surprised and disappointed later to discover that the young black caddy I had employed had taken a few dollars from my bag. Maybe it should be expected but I had given him a generous tip and some golf gear including a baseball cap which seemed to mean more to him than the money.

Around the middle of the month I had an experience that I hope I will never have to experience again. February 17th will be forever etched in my mind as it proved to be one of the most challenging days I have had since I arrived here. It began innocently enough as the previous night was quieter than usual. I had given most of the staff a day off as a result and had allowed Mika to go Tsumeb to get his car sorted as it was giving him problems. Our chef was also off and I was getting ready for a quiet evening just around 5.00pm. It was actually raining pretty hard and there was thunder and lightening in the air. The lightening storms here are amazing and unlike anything we see at home. The power went as a result and I was beginning to think about cranking up the backup generator. However I then realised we were low on diesel but no panic as there was just me and I could manage one night in the dark if necessary. Not five minutes later a bus pulled up at the lodge gate and ten German visitors and a guide called Tutu ran in out of the rain. Tutu has been here many times and is the image of Frank Bruno. I nearly died as they were clearly here to stay and were expecting a warm Ghaub welcome! Instead they received a shocked what are you doing here! I managed to cover up reasonably well and thinking on my feet figured out that someone had made a big mistake but this wasn't the time to find out who was responsible. I had to pretend that we were expecting them, rush of to prepare welcome drinks and plan what I was going to do with no chef, no power and no staff! It was such a shock when you are sort of switching off for the evening and then have to kick back into gear. Luckily I had Klaus, one of the new staff who can drive and I sent him off quickly to look for Christofine, our chef. I explained to the guests that dinner would be a little later than usual this evening at 8.00pm but at that moment in time I wasn't sure there would be any dinner at all. Having shown the guests to their rooms which thankfully were cleaned earlier and ready my next problem was to get the generator working as darkness was closing in fast. Meanwhile Klaus was returning from the staff location with the chef even though she was off duty and could easily have been in Tsumeb visiting her family. I had to drive then to the farm to look for diesel and when I got there the place was in darkness and no sign of Billy. Everything was locked up for the night and my stress levels were rising. I eventually found one of the farm workers who helped me siphon diesel out of one of the trucks as the rain came pelting down and my panic grew. Quick dash back to the lodge, checked out the kitchen, got the generator on with help, set the tables quickly, two minutes to wash and change and then appear Basil like full of charm just in time to greet the guests with a pre meal gin and tonic! There have been many occasions when I felt like this was closer to Fawlty Towers than I would care to admit and this was certainly one of them. There just wasn't time to panic and I was on auto pilot for the remainder of the evening. I was ready to fall into bed at 10.00pm which is usually the time guests choose to retire but this night of all nights four of the guests with Tutu's encouragement decided to enjoy their last night of the tour and stayed up drinking till 12.30am.They also wanted breakfast at 7.00am and I knew I would have to be up at 6.00am or earlier to help prepare it. The bus pulled away at 8.00am on the dot next morning and I breathed a sigh of relief. I would never want to go through an evening like that again. We still haven't decided who was responsible for cancelling the booking. It could only have been myself or Mika. We can joke about it now but at the time it was a nightmare. I still think it was him. He thinks it was me. He is usually right. You can decide.

During the month I was also shocked to read in the local paper about a plane crash at Windhoek's second airport involving a light aircraft. The pilot was a German/Namibian called Keuckie who owns The Rostock Ritz lodge near Solitaire. Most of my Irish friends that have travelled to Namibia over the past year have stayed at Rostock as it is a beautiful location out in the desert and Keuckie has become a good friend. He is still in a critical condition and was lucky to survive apparently. I am sure anyone who has met him would be interested in his progress and I will keep you informed.

Had another lovely English couple stay with us recently and the English continue to be my favourite guests. The language helps but it is more than that. They are generally polite and appreciative and intrigued to find an Irishman out here in the sticks. English visitors just want to enjoy their holiday and have a good time. I met Doreen and Ken in the queue at Gatwick coming out after Christmas. We got chatting and they told me they spend three months in Namibia every year usually during the English winter. They were a lovely couple and although both in their late 60's could have passed for ten years younger. We had a good chat and I invited them to come to stay at Ghaub. Well they rang during the month and had two days with us when we chatted late into the night and they shared stories of their travels over the years which were incredible. They will now send friends back to Ghaub soon. I suppose that's all part of marketing and taking opportunities to introduce people to your lodge. The trick is in getting people here as once they see the place they are generally impressed. Now I talk to people all the time and carry some brochures with me whenever I am travelling. Same happened when Greg from England and Naomi came to stay. I decided to get a new satellite dish recently too after going a full year without a TV. The main reason was to have television for stay over guests who are here for several nights as they usually like to stay in touch with the news on the BBC world service. Sky is also freely available here and you can pick up the sports channels from around the world. It is also handy for children to watch cartoons when their parents are having a leisurely dinner. It only cost N$1,000.00 to install the dish and we pay N$400.00 per month which is good value for seventy stations. I haven't had time to watch it too often myself but will be able to keep in touch with what's happening in the world from now on. Perhaps it's best not to know.

My Offaly friends arrived on Saturday 21st February and I picked them up as arranged from the airport. Jimmy from Clara, Johnny from Ferbane, Martin from Rahan and Christy and his wife Kathleen from Kilcormac. Johnny actually told them that he wasn't coming but he flew in from Johannesburg just before they arrived from London. We set it up that he would get lost behind a newspaper in the restaurant and after I greeted the others I brought them for a quick cup of coffee before we hit the road. Looking for seats I asked this gentleman would he mind if we joined him and when Johnny took down the paper it was the first of many surprises for them. I was really chuffed to see them all after months of planning and to get the chance to share the country with them. We had a long drive north in two cars and stopped for lunch in my favourite stop off point at Okahandja Country lodge for lunch. There is a typical African feel about the place and it's a good introduction for new arrivals. The gang stayed four nights at the lodge in total before I packed them off to see a bit of the country. There were many highlights and laughs along the way. I was really looking forward to taking them to the Maria Bronn on the Sunday for church and it didn't disappoint. The children were in great voice and the service was an incredible celebration. The nuns were delighted to meet my Irish friends and interested to discover were all Irish people a bit mad! We were asked to stay afterwards as the children had prepared a concert especially for us. Words could not describe the next two hours as we were treated to a dance competition, a singing contest and a Miss Maria Bronn pageant which was judged by a panel like the X factor. The Simon Cowell character was very convincing. The photographs certainly don't do it justice but it was a treat for the Biffos and I enjoyed it immensely as well. I am only a Biffo when it suits me. We had a great few days and I can safely say that County Offaly can be proud of their foreign ambassadors and the good humour they brought to Africa. The gang headed west last Wednesday after four nights and I will meet up with them in Windhoek next week before they head home. No doubt they will have stories to tell as they wear their Irishness proudly wherever they go.

At this stage I am beginning to think of my journey home in early April and the end of this particular part of this amazing adventure. I will leave here on April 2nd after an incredible fifteen months or so but will stay involved and keep in close contact with Mika and the staff from my base in Ireland. Who knows what the future holds but I could happily live here perhaps when the lads are older. I have decided to return to work in the Rutland at least on a part-time basis from April 14th. I will keep my interest in the lodge and farm and hopefully return with Marian and family at some future stage. If anyone told me two years ago I would spend the best part of fifteen months in Africa I would have sent for the men in the white coats-and I don't mean the umpires! It was the last thing on my mind when we came here on holiday two years ago but I wouldn't have missed it for a moment -and it's not over yet. I feel privileged to be here and despite numerous personal challenges along the way I wouldn't have changed too much. For anyone in a position to travel to Africa looking for a unique experience then jump at the chance of visiting Namibia. I could never describe what it is really like. You would just have to experience it for yourself.

14

THE ONLY LIMITS ARE THE LIMITS OF OUR IMAGINATIONS

As March comes to a close I am reaching the end of this part of the journey and now counting down the days. It is with a heavy heart but also with excitement that I sit here trying to describe the most recent escapades and adventures that have come my way. I am so looking forward to coming home to be with my family as I have missed them all terribly at times even allowing for my short trips home. However I will also leave part of my soul here. I have spoken about moments of clarity, about moments of deep contentment and feelings of finally catching up with myself. Becoming the person I wanted to be seemed so out of reach and truthfully it's a never ending journey. But I have moved further along the path without a doubt.

In attempting to summarize the time here in some sort of coherent way I feel I must list just some of my main achievements if you can bear with me. Firstly I am still alive! I haven't killed anyone. I haven't set the place on fire or rolled the car. I haven't been arrested although I came close twice and there is still time! The latest run in with the law I will explain later and it's all Mick Hanley's fault! I haven't let the Irish down and can safely say the locals here now have an awareness about all things Irish. I wear my Irishness like a badge and take every opportunity to promote the country and the Irish people. It's true when the Irish are working abroad they seem to become more conscious of their homeland. I have discovered a new appreciation for Irish music and now listen regularly to Paul Brady, Frances Black, Van Morrison, U 2, The Fureys, The Dubliners, Sinead O Connor, and some lesser names like Mundy, The Blades and The Dialectics. I would guess the last named are a new name for most. I actually picked up a CD of theirs from Anthony some months ago. They are a local group that busk in Grafton Street some Saturdays and they do some great covers. Their CD sounds like it was recorded in someone's garage but I like the roughness and rawness of it and they can really play. Any passengers that I carry just have to get used to the music and they are slowly coming round.

I also have a baseball cap in the Irish colours and I wear it like a crown. I take great umbrage whenever I am confused for an English man or asked when I am travelling home to the UK. There isn't a horse high enough to get down from at times like that. I put them straight fairly sharply and give them a brief History and Geography lesson for the price of one.

I forgot to mention that our second cook Johanna had a surprise for us last month. She was expecting a baby in April and was clearly heavily pregnant since Christmas but managing. She actually worked her usual Monday shift at the beginning of the month and prepared dinner for nine guests. The following morning Mika knocked at my door at 5.00am to tell me that Johanna had pains during the night and needed to see the Doctor. I suggested that Immanuel take her into town straight away to the hospital just in case as we are quite remote here. At 9.30am she gave birth to twin baby boys! It was a shock to everyone especially Johanna herself as her last scan had failed to pick up two babies and her due date was still two months away. Thankfully Mother and babies are doing well but we could have had an emergency here at the farm. Just one more event that could only happen here and I still struggle to believe that Johanna could be working one evening and just ten hours later she is sitting up in hospital ringing us with her news.

At the beginning of March I decided to tell the staff at our first Monday meeting that I would be going home on April 2nd. Their reaction was very interesting and surprising. They were in shock for a while as they had no idea I was planning to leave. I wanted to give them enough time but not too much time to get used to the idea and prepare for a new person coming in. Some of the staff were quite emotional and there were some tears which really shook me. I think their main concern was that their conditions would change under a different manager or that their jobs might be at risk. I reassured them that very little would change and that we would not be selling the farm. When I explained how much I missed my family and had to return to work to provide for them they were much more understanding. Family is so important here and everyone appreciates that it always comes first. Now they are getting used to the idea but still a bit concerned that a new person will change the working atmosphere that exists. I really have no complaints about their willingness to work and their reliability. They are all dedicated and can be trusted to do what has to be done with just a little direction. We have a good team now and I am delighted that our three newest recruits that I took on earlier in the year are working out really well. Andreas continues to surprise me and has turned into a very capable and courteous waiter. The guests enjoy chatting with him and I often smile to myself when I overhear him explaining Kavango customs to a captive European audience and remember the shy, nervous young man who arrived for a job interview just twelve months ago.

We had a lovely visit from Stephen and Breda from Kildare during the past month too. Friends of my sister Evelyn and also partners in the business they stayed with us for four nights before heading off to see some of the sights. I was looking forward to taking them to the Maria Bronn school as I do with all my visitors from home. It was a very special occasion as the children and nuns gave us a special warm welcome. They seem to know when I have guests coming as they seem to add an extra dimension to the service. My Offaly friends had brought over two sets of Jerseys for the children in February and we were now treated on this occasion to a parade of the football team and the netball team kitted out in their Leinster Play station gear including socks, shorts and blue jerseys that looked very smart. They marched in formation singing songs of celebration encouraged by the nuns. We could have stayed for hours if we had time but we did get some great footage and photographs that will be treasured. Stephen and Breda had a ball and I think they enjoyed their trip generally. They managed to fit in The Etosha National Park, the Africat Foundation, Swakopmund, Cape Cross and Andre's farm during their stay. I think they will also return.

I also took an overnight trip to Oshakati recently which is in the far North West of the country not far from the Angolan border. I was invited by the Sisters who have a convent there as they wanted to thank me for the help we have given to the Maria Bronn School in Grootfontein. I was curious about Oshakati having heard so much about it and was conscious that time was running out so this might be the last opportunity for a while to visit a different part of the country. It is about a three hundred kilometre drive North West from the lodge but mostly on good tar roads. It turned out to be an education as it's very different to Tsumeb, Grootfontein and other Namibian towns closer to the lodge. It's in fact more like the Africa you would expect from TV images with wandering animals on the roads, overcrowded streets and generally organized chaos. They had serious flooding not long ago which seems to be an annual event and much of the countryside was under several feet of water with lots of people fishing in pools by the roadside with an array of homemade nets and selling their catch to passers by. The journey was eventful in itself as when the sisters heard I was travelling up I was joined by three elderly nuns and a young ten year old girl whose uncle had passed away and it was an opportunity for her to return home for the funeral. I gathered that nobody told her why she was going home which must have been confusing for her but one of the sisters explained to me that in their culture it is best to hear that kind of news from an immediate family member. Driving for three hours with a full car of passengers with very little English can be a real challenge! I hadn't much time to prepare but luckily decided to leave my heavy metal music behind! One sister chewed on a sweat potato which was the size of a large turnip for most of the journey. After an hour in silence I passed round copies of Halo magazine and Nuns weekly! Only joking. But I did find myself for some reason thinking up the crudest jokes. It was a bit surreal but interesting and it was noticeable that all the passengers became more animated as we crossed the line into Ovamboland which is their homeland. Oshakati would never win a tidy towns competition as it was obvious on first impressions that this was indeed a different Africa to anywhere I had visited previously. The noise hit me first as we drove in and the crowds of people milling round reminded me of a scene from footage of an old African black and white film I had once seen but can't remember the name. It looked a bit like the long mile road in Dublin with buildings either side of a long street that seemed to stretch forever. That was the town pretty much with one large street with colourful street markets and disorganised taxi ranks. I spent the evening watching the Sound of Music, which somehow had found its way from Grootfontein, with five Sisters after an interesting dinner prepared by the sisters themselves consisting of scrambled eggs, porridge and chicken portions. The comments were hilarious as Sr Maria or Julie Andrews battled with her feelings for Captain Von Trapp. It became clear very quickly that we were also now in Mosquito country as I swatted miniature flies that buzzed around us all evening and got bitten once through my jeans which was a bit of a shock. Until then I had not been bitten by anything in over twelve months since I arrived in the country. The next morning I was taken on a tour of the town and the flooded areas and received a few funny looks which I also had not experienced before. There was definitely a slightly hostile reaction from some locals who were trying to figure out what I was doing there. I think my presence was more acceptable because I was with the sisters and may have been confused for a pastor or padre. The flooded areas were incredible as large areas were completely submerged and small farms and holdings were washed away with the tide. Despite promises from the government to correct the problem the situation will probably be repeated next year and beyond. This is the heart of Ovamboland and the birthplace of many from the Ruling Swapo party but it seems that once power is assumed that the leaders neglect their own and aid is not reaching the areas in most need. It was a flying visit and I was glad to have the opportunity of adding Oshakati to the places I have visited but would not recommend it for inclusion on a list of must see places for tourists coming to Namibia.

There was a terrible tragedy during March which really affected me. I have become friendly with a local Namibian/German couple who live nearby in Otavi and are involved in the Khorab Lodge and also have the local agency for Avis car rental. I have rented cars from them several times since I have been here and some of my visiting friends have also met with Alonka and Jan. I heard through the grapevine that they were off work but nobody was saying why until I heard from a neighbour that one of their twin boys aged six had died in a tragic accident on their farm. Alonka and Jan had stayed at Ghaub with the kids more than once and the boys were beautiful blue eyed blonds and full of fun. Apparently one of the kids fell off the back of a buggy at their home and died on the way to the hospital. I was devastated to hear about it and could only imagine what Jan and Alonka were going through. I still haven't spoken to them and really won't know what to say. I don't know how anyone could recover from such a tragedy. It's just so incredibly sad.

You remember last time I also mentioned Keuckie from Rostock Ritz lodge had a plane accident and was in intensive care for a month. He is now off the critical list and is making a slow recovery. His partner contacted me last week and said that he was improving but that his recovery would be a long and slow process but they were now more hopeful that he would be able to return to work in time. I have invited him to Ghaub if he needs a quiet place to recuperate at any stage during his rehabilitation. I hope to keep in touch with him whatever he decides after I return home. The Offaly gang visited Rostock during their trip and it was one of their favourite lodges. Well worth a visit if you are coming to Namibia.

On a lighter note I have been trying to breed chickens over the past month with mixed results. I bought a cockerel off one of the staff at the farm which in itself was an experience. I went up early one Tuesday and it took us twenty minutes to catch him! He wasn't a bit happy and kept strutting off into the bushes. I named him Mick Jagger there and then. We eventually trapped him and tied his legs together and he gave out stink all the way back to the lodge. After introducing him to his new home he settled down and perhaps realised that having fourteen hens to himself wasn't so bad after all. Christo Hand from Kilcormac was here at the time and he marked my card as to what to do in order to extend the family. He has a lot of experience in the birds and the bees from his days in the E.S.B! Christy was convinced that unless Mick Jagger was gay that we should have some chicks within three weeks which was a surprise to me. The staff were very sceptical but lo and behold on Sunday March 15th when putting in the hens for the night I heard this cheep cheep cheep coming from the box and was thrilled to find this day old chick pecking around looking for food even though she was only hours old. Hard to believe that she could fit inside an egg that morning. We now have two chicks and waiting for more but I think Mick Jagger is misfiring- a bit like the Offaly forwards!

St Patrick's Day came and went this year and really it was just another regular day. Last year I did make an effort and put up some bunting and explained the significance of St Patrick's Day to the staff. This year though I had an early start with guests and worked late into the evening as well so there was no time for celebration. My thoughts were in Croke Park throughout the afternoon as I knew Kilmacud Crokes were playing in the All Ireland Club final and the manager Paddy Carr has been a good friend for years. I was delighted to find out later on the Hogan stand website that Crokes had won and pleased particularly for Paddy. Sometimes the good guys do finish first.

We had an amazing incident on the farm two weeks ago when poachers were intercepted near the western boundary fence and a cross country chase followed with an interesting outcome. Billy and a neighbouring farmer finally caught up with them half way up the mountain and seemingly there was a shoot out which shocked me. Apparently as poaching is considered such a serious offence one is entitled to defend one's property and livestock if you are fired at first. Eventually the guys ran off through the bushes leaving behind a small car and trailer with two large Kudus and two warthogs in the back. The police were called, the car impounded and they were able to trace the owner of the car easily by checking their records. Billy ended up giving the meat to the police which is how business is done here as they will now be quicker to respond to any future calls. However yesterday Billy told me that the impounded car was seen driving around Tsumeb and it seems that the police may be in cahoots with the poachers! No real surprise there either as you never really know who to trust here. This brings me back eventually to the Mick Hanley story I mentioned earlier. Mick, brother of David, who used to front the Morning Ireland programme on RTE Radio, and former lead singer with Moving Hearts and Rusty Old Halo has always been a favourite of mine. An excellent songwriter who has written for Mary Black and others, he is also a terrific singer as well and really for me captures the mood of a song. I think it was Frank Foley, brother of Kevin who scored what's considered the best goal of all time for Meath in Croke Park in 1991 against Dublin, who introduced Mick Hanley's music to me originally many years ago. I have had this CD for years of Rusty Old Halo which I always carry when travelling and never tire of it. Anyway months ago I was in this small coffee shop in Tsumeb that plays the Country music and I got to know the owner and gave him this CD as well as one of Nanci Griffith's and one of Frances Black's, other favourites of mine. I got Nancy and Frances back a while ago but when I was in town recently and as I am travelling home soon I decided to ask for the Rusty Old Halo CD back. The owner was out and the local manager who I knew reasonably well from dropping in refused to hand it over without clearing it with the owner first. Fair enough I thought but then when I thought about it a bit longer I felt the guy was doubting what I was saying. I went back to discuss it with him and he refused point blank to budge even though I could see the CD on the shelf and doubted if it was played since the last time I was in. I have to admit then I got thick about it and told the guy I was prepared to be reasonable but would be calling in later after I finished the shopping and would expect to be taking the CD home with me. When I dropped back in half an hour later he again refused to budge and called an off duty policeman who just happened to be having a coffee nearby to sort out the situation. Now this was the most unlikely looking police officer you could imagine and the smell of alcohol off him would have knocked a horse. He looked about twenty years of age and if it wasn't for his badge I would have thought that he was having a laugh. Anyway it was no great surprise to me that he took the other guy's side and suggested that I come back when the owner was there. I was tempted to argue the point and create a scene but decided to let it go and now Mick Hanley will gather dust in a small café in Tsumeb until I come back in August perhaps. I may have time to have another try to retrieve what is mine before I go home as I can be a bit like a dog with a bone sometimes. It drives me crazy when I think I am experiencing an injustice of if my honesty is been questioned. As Mick might say or sing-"I'm up and I'm walking around but I'm still not cured"!!

I missed the Irish Wales rugby match which was so annoying as we have a satellite dish now and I actually saw the Scottish match last week. I forgot to pay the monthly bill and we were cut off on the Friday and with Independence Day on Saturday everything closes down for the week-end. Delighted to read about Irish boxer Bernard Dunne as well as I always thought he would be World Champion one day. I remember watching one of his earliest professional fights in a small pub in Donegal on a golfing week-end with brothers Paul, Stan and good friend Neil O Sullivan a couple of years ago. Good week-end all round for Irish sport and I am sure it will give the whole country a badly needed lift. I am beginning to think that I am a jinx when it comes to watching Irish sport as Harrington has won three majors now since I have been here and I didn't see a shot. Now with the grand slam maybe I should stop watching as I only bring bad luck. I'll test the theory over the next twelve months before deciding. Independence Day by the way was also a quiet affair here although there were parades in the bigger towns and speeches broadcast from the President and other leading politicians remembering those who fought for Namibia's independence. The politics here is still a little confusing as the ruling Swapo party enjoy a large majority and seem to undermine the RDP, who seem to be their closest opposition, at every opportunity. Anyone in public office who speaks out publicly against the Swapo Government seems to be removed from their position. It does raise some concern about the future as one strong dominant ruling party can influence change which is not always progressive or inclusive. The Swapo Youth also seem to be quite militant and makes you wonder about the long term future for minorities here. For now it seems the country is stable and the system is working well. Apart from one or two isolated incidents I can honestly say that I have been treated very well here and have always felt safe. There is a relaxed atmosphere everywhere you go and travelling is easy throughout the country. Many guests have commented to me about how safe they feel driving through the country over wide stretches of uninhabited land.

Last July I bought a horse from a Dr Maas from Otjiwarongo for N$5,000 or less than Five Hundred Euro and she was a bargain. Charmaine is an eight year old mare and despite having a fall off her she has turned into a fine looking horse with a better temperament than her owner! At the time I offered Dr Maas a night at the lodge with his wife and children as a sweetener in the deal as I felt it was only fair and he might also bring friends back to the lodge if he enjoyed his stay. He eventually took up the offer this month and booked in for a Saturday night with his family. I had said to him to bring his children thinking he might have three or possibly four as families here are typically on the small side. He arrived with eight of his ten children, his wife and his mother-in-law! I tell the story against myself as I found it funny and a reminder again that to assume makes an ass of you and me! It turned out that they all enjoyed their stay immensely and Dr Maas was so happy and thrilled with the condition of the mare that he offered me two more horses in exchange for another complimentary week-end. So it pays to be reasonable sometimes and it now looks like we will have two new additions to our growing equestrian team before the end of the month.

I am looking forward to next week-end as I have invited all the Compion family to Ghaub as it will be the last week-end before I return home. For most of them it will be their first time to see the lodge and I am hoping for a favourable reaction. The place looks really well at the moment as the rains stopped last week and it's beginning to get really warm again. The landscape is green and lush and it's possibly the best time of the year to travel as in a few weeks the landscape will be very dry and burned looking and there won't be rain for another six months. Hard to believe but true. It's not even as if it might rain occasionally. You can be sure there won't be a drop until November at least. We have started having barbecues again which the guests usually enjoy and will definitely have one for the extended family next Saturday evening. I hope to have a get together with the staff before I go home as well. Next Wednesday I will head for Windhoek and begin the journey home. I usually stay one night in Windhoek just I case something goes wrong on the way down as you never know here what can delay you. Still no definite news on a replacement manager to support Mika in my absence. I interviewed a few people and thought last week I may have found the right person. A lady from Swakop who had a good background in catering and was fluent in German and several other languages seemed like a strong candidate. I spoke to her on the phone and she seemed personable and we arranged to meet with her and Andre in Okahandja as I was travelling down to Windhoek. She cancelled at the last minute as she couldn't arrange a lift although she did get to speak with Andre over the phone and he was hopeful that she could be the right person for us. I arranged to meet her on the way back northwards the following day instead but was immediately under whelmed. She just didn't impress or strike me as someone capable of carrying the responsibilities of the lodge without a lot of support. We had to start looking again and then by chance on Sunday last after the Maria Bronn service I met another friend from the Bank in Grootfontein who has always been helpful when I needed assistance with the challenges banking presents. His brother was looking for a job having been retrenched from a large lodge in the South. He is moving to the Grootfontein area with his family and it sounded like a real opportunity. I invited them out to the lodge that afternoon for a chat and to show them round. I then rang Andre and asked him to check the guys history with his previous employers and find out why he was been retrenched. His wife is an accomplished cook which could be interesting but I am really not sure. I was left feeling uneasy after their visit despite their credentials and obvious interest in the position. I found them quite disrespectful towards the staff and unfortunately they came across like some of the German/Namibian white people that I have encountered here who are quite judgemental towards the black people generally. That won't work for me as Mika and the staff are our best assets. Whoever we find will have to fit in with the relaxed but respectful working atmosphere that we have introduced.

There have been many highlights over the past fifteen months and I now have memories that will last a lifetime. It has been the best time and yet in ways the most difficult thing I have ever done. I have missed the family so much at times that there were days I nearly cracked up. Especially during the early days it was almost unbearable and I thought this was a big mistake. I never quite despaired because I always believed that this was meant to happen and wouldn't end in tears. The best times were when friends came out to visit from Ireland and I was able to share the experience with them. I will never forget all those who did travel to Namibia and I honestly believe that they had memorable holidays. The lodge continues to excite me as we make improvements here and there. The reaction from guests is still extremely affirming and we seemingly compare well with all the leading lodges that are included in the itineraries of the major operators. Even Namibians who have lived here all their lives talk about the uniqueness of Ghaub and the magic of the setting.

I have received so much kindness from so many sources that I can't begin to thank people. The greatest gift I have received has been the friendship of the staff and children of The Maria Bronn School. Without a doubt my Sunday visits became the highlight of my week and in ways it has restored my faith in the church. I really do think that it's time to hand over the reins of the Church to the Sisters and nuns as the priests and bishops for me have failed to show example or leadership and have got distracted by power and wealth. Let the Sisters have a go and perhaps they can rescue a sinking ship. I have never met such selfless dedication from an incredible group of spiritual people working with limited resources. The children clearly feel safe and cared for. I hope to continue my association with the school for a long time whatever happens and help in small ways to improve their lot. Already they have given me far more than anything I could give back in return. The singing and dancing are out of this world and I would like to be able to bring them all to Ireland and put them on the Late Late show or some other such stage to show Irish people what real talent and humility is about.

I have also loved the wildlife during my time here and the day to day closeness with animals and nature. From the unconditional ever presence of a dog which remains a constant shadow, something I never experienced before to the daily surprise of encountering a wild animal in close proximity has lifted my spirit more than once. I enjoyed hanging around with the horses and learning to ride even at this relatively late stage of my life. Horses definitely have an energy and an awareness about them that sets them apart from other animals. Horse sense should never be underestimated. It's what stops them betting on people! The bird life here is also a special feature and I can honestly say that I have never really noticed birds before now. I have never liked the idea of caged birds anywhere and can't understand why anyone would keep a caged bird as a pet or companion. I have taken some fantastic pictures of birds around the lodge in recent weeks. My favourite is one of a giant eagle owl that happened to come into the garden late one evening about two weeks ago and could be identified by his high pitched call. He stayed around for a few days before moving on.

The Namibian people are fascinating in many ways and the variety of cultures and customs would take years to fully appreciate and understand. The country seems crowded at times and yet remains one of the most under populated countries in the world by comparison. I read recently that size wise Namibia compares with France and the UK put together which gives you some idea of the vastness of the country. To imagine all that with just a population half as much as the total population of Ireland gives one a better idea what a unique country Namibia is. The people have an amazing gift for languages and the average person seems to have a good understanding of at least three different dialects.

I have learned so much from the staff here and marvel at their positive outlook to life and their determination to improve their positions with hard work and dedication. They are so tolerant and patient -traits that I am trying to acquire but still have a long way to go to come close to matching their resolve. Nothing seems too big a problem and anything is possible. I have been reminded how western values differ so much from African values that I feel hypocritical and a fraud at times. They look up to me when really I have little to teach them. The people have a great ability to accept loss or bad news with grace. I honestly think that many African kids with very little are happier than Irish kids with too much. Simple tastes and a simple way of life with no pressure to keep up with your neighbour sums up the mindset here.

The business is going well and the lodge and farm are flying. I hope to stay involved closely from home. It would be heart breaking to see the place disintegrate or go backwards after so much time and hard work. I plan to return in August for a few weeks and then hopefully in time when the lads are older to make a new home here. Thanks to everyone for your messages and e-mails which were much appreciated at difficult times. They gave me strength when I needed it and was doubting this whole venture. Looking forward to catching up soon.

15

A ROOSTER ONE DAY, A FEATHER DUSTER THE NEXT

I returned to Ireland in early April and went back to work as planned to my old job as a counsellor at the Rutland Centre after Easter. I was nervous about returning and meeting all my former colleagues again as really I believed that I could be leaving for good sixteen months previously. I had also spent time serving drinks and waiting on tables during my break away which could not have been more different to life in the Rutland. I was also concerned that maybe I would have lost the enthusiasm for the work and would never recapture it. The years of negativity and resistance may have taken its toll and perhaps I was in a for a very rude awakening. However as it happened I quickly realised that I returned energised and refreshed and faced the work with a new enthusiasm. I actually now believe that the break has been invaluable and has provided me with an impetus and an opportunity to stretch myself and bring me to a heightened awareness that can only strengthen my ability to be present for the clients. For now I am more available and less busy in my head which can only improve the quality of my work. I feel different and more at ease with myself and with life in general. It's difficult to describe but my experiences over the past fifteen months have forced me to re-evaluate what I was doing and appraise both my personal and my working life. I have learned so much from the incredible people that I worked closely with in Namibia that I intend to try to challenge myself to push myself harder and realise my full potential within the guidelines of my role as a counsellor. I have changed undoubtedly and have found my voice again as well as a quiet determination to honour what I believe in and to follow my heart.

I would like to think that perhaps my story might encourage others to follow their heart too and perhaps satisfy any longings that dwell somewhere in the background. I don't wish to tell anyone how to live their life. I certainly don't have all the answers and can only share my own experience. Not everyone could take off for a year without the support of their partner no matter what opportunity presented itself. I was lucky to be able to make a major career and lifestyle change and choice because others made it possible for me. Sometimes you have to follow your gut and trust that things will work out as long as you are true to yourself and honest in your efforts. I was concerned that this might all sound a bit self indulgent and I certainly would not want that to be the case. I can safely say that I have no regrets about the decision I made. Even though there were tough times and moments when I questioned my sanity I would change very little. I feel like I have finally caught up with myself and grown into the person I want to become. Maybe others won't notice any difference but that's not the most important thing. I know and that's all that matters. I have always got by with a little ability and a lot of hard work. This chapter of my life is coming to an end and I am excited about what the future holds.

I was to return to Ghaub in August for a three week break after four months back home. I decided to bring Gareth with me as in truth he wouldn't have allowed me to travel without him again. Of all the family members he is the one who has been bowled over by Namibia like his Dad and I made the familiar journey once again. It was interesting returning this time as it was going to be a working holiday as I wanted to give Mika some time off. We did plan a short visit to the Caprivi area in the north east as I always wanted to see that part of the country having heard so much about it. We received a terrific welcome back from the staff and the animals! It was obvious that Mika had made sure to have everything looking spotless for us and I was genuinely moved by the reception we received and the effort that was obviously made. Apart from commenting on how much weight I had gained in four months I could have no complaints. They were right too as despite my best intentions

I had slowly drifted back into my old routines of watching too much television, comfort eating and not taking enough exercise. The difference between Irish and African lifestyle was again evident as I had never felt better than when I was in Namibia for the previous year and was back to my football playing day's weight of twenty five years ago. I make promises to myself to start again when I get back. Bono recognised us immediately and was extremely excited. He hardly left my side for the duration of our stay and camped outside our room. Gareth was in his element and reacquainted himself with the staff and the surroundings as he went exploring with Bono following close behind. Our three days in the north was very enjoyable and we got to visit Namushasha Lodge which is located on the way to Livingston near Victoria Falls. My favourite stop off was the Kaisosi lodge on the Kavango river which divides Namibia and Angola. Such a beautiful place and full of character and steeped in history. We enjoyed a late afternoon fishing trip on the river and retired to our typically African styled accommodation to the sounds of hippos grunting in the nearby reeds. I spent the bulk of our trip working at the lodge and threw myself back into the early mornings and long days with enthusiasm. The staff were as hard working as always. Gareth enjoyed the banter and learned more about African customs thanks to Klaus and Andreas particularly who took time to include him in their conversations.

I decided that the lodge needed a bit of colour and promised to buy some plants and flowers to brighten up the grounds now that Winter was coming to an end. I had to go into Grootfontein to the Bank and to do some shopping and so called into the only garden centre in town. Gareth had stayed behind to rest as he had been too excited to sleep properly for the first three days of our visit. A helpful, friendly local gentleman helped me pick out some plants with instant colour which were least likely to appeal to the visiting animals who ramble in to the garden after dark. When I went inside to fix up for the shrubs I nearly stepped on the most beautiful little pup that I ever saw which was curled up in a ball fast asleep. Then another little ball of wool made a bee line for us before tripping over himself as he was running too fast for his short stumpy legs! I was smitten straight away and offered to give the two pups a good home at the lodge. Their owner and shrewd businessman who was also the gardener knew their worth as they were pure bred Bull terriers and refused my first offer. I was thinking of a pal for Bono and Gareth's reaction if I returned with a pup. I eventually persuaded the man to part with one of the pups and paid him too much but nevertheless was happy enough with the deal. More excitement greeted me as I returned with much interest on the latest addition to the Ghaub family from the staff, Gareth and Bono-in that order. We settled on Buster as an appropriate name although I had another of those what am I after doing moments later in the afternoon as I contemplated leaving another responsibility to Mika after we returned home again the following week. I thought it best to put him in straight away with Bono for the night and trust that they would get on as otherwise he might prove too much of a nuisance and I might have to return him back to his previous shrewd owner! Luckily they got on famously and another crisis was averted and Buster was here to stay. The guests were smitten like me and Buster seemed to have an inbuilt sense of how to attract attention and an appreciation of his own importance.

I worked hard for the few weeks and Mika had a well deserved break and we at least made progress in recruiting a manager who would share the duties with Mika. I spoke to Andre during his visit about a young guy I met earlier in the year at another lodge who was looking for work. Wilson was the closest guy to Mika that I had met and impressed me with his attitude and manner whenever I met him as I used to bump into him in town from time to time. We decided to contact him and check whether or not he was still looking for work and I rang him on the off chance. He responded favourably straight away and we agreed that Andre would meet him the following week. I am hopeful that Wilson may prove to be the person we are looking for. He is a Damara chap with excellent English and good people skills and I think he and Mika will work well together.

I was never really in favour of a Namibian or German manager coming in over Mika as he has proved himself to be more than capable of carrying the responsibility of managing the lodge and dealing with the operators and guests. This could be the best bit of business that we do during this trip.

We head home after three weeks as Gareth starts back to school and I have to return to work. Overall it has been most enjoyable but I have a strange inkling that just maybe I am losing my grip on Ghaub and my life is about to change once more. I can't explain it fully but this time I want to take in the sights and go for a long walk through the farm before we leave. The future is still uncertain but some of the partners are less enthralled with this whole adventure than I have been and as the recession bites at home we may have to consider our position. This could not have happened without the help of friends and family and I would hate a situation if it became a financial burden to anyone or if the partners lost out on their investment. It was so much more than an investment or business opportunity for me but I have to consider everyone's position and be sensible for a change! I returned to work again feeling energised after our trip. It feels like a boost to the batteries and friends have noticed that I seem to be in a different place within myself after my trips. Despite all the positives I find myself thinking about the reality of life in Namibia for many of its inhabitants. Although the country is now self determined and since Independence the standard of living has improved hugely for many, there remains a shockingly poor health care system which needs urgent attention. Although the hospitals seem to be well staffed with willing and caring personnel their training and experience appear to be inadequate in order to provide primary care. I am stunned at the number of infant casualties during my time in the country and that is only among the people I came into direct contact with. I mentioned earlier that Frieda one of the girls who works in the laundry lost her daughter Beyozetha after a long illness when she was just three years old. Just before I returned in August Mika contacted me with the terribly sad news that both of Johanna's twins, two boys born last January had died within two days of each other after a short unexplained illness. There had been such excitement when her twins were born earlier in the year as they were premature but seemed healthy and strong. My first call in August was to drop into Johanna to pay my respects and it was a difficult visit. I felt so sorry for her. She was devastated and yet had a remarkable acceptance of God's will which I have noticed here before but struggle to come to terms with it. During our trip in August Mika took Ida and her little daughter Antonett, called after our Anthony, to hospital as she had been unwell for a number of weeks. The diagnosis mentioned fluid on the brain and the prognosis was poor. Mika contacted after I arrived home to tell me that Antonett had also passed. For three members of the staff to lose infants in such a short time puts everything into perspective for me. It's partly the harsh reality of life here but an indictment on the system and the lack of intent on behalf of the government to bring standards up to the required level as it appears that there is more than enough finance to improve health care but it is not been directed into the proper channels. You read in the local papers about millions of dollars been spent on a Presidential palace in Windhoek and new government buildings and top of the range cars for government ministers. I struggle with frustration and ask myself more than once does my presence here support an unequal system or does it challenge the inequalities. It depends who you talk to and we certainly cannot pass judgement or suggest that the Irish system is perfect. I still believe that I would have picked up some signs of contempt or judgement from the local people in certain situations I have been in if I was considered in any way a mercenary or opportunist. I have always been treated with warmth and genuine friendliness and Mika assures me that the people he meets and knows consider people like me to be fortunate but never in a resentful envious way.

Now we are back a few weeks and my inklings regarding the future of the lodge and farm are turning out to be correct. It is beginning to look like the majority of the shareholders are eager to sell if the offer is right and I may have to accept that we may not after all relocate to Africa when the lads are older. It is possible that Andre will agree to buy the property himself and take over the running of the business and make his own future here at Ghaub. If that's the outcome the staff will be happy that their own futures will be secure. How ironic it would be if Andre ends up moving his family three hundred miles north to a farm that his Irish cousins found on a family holiday two years previously to Namibia where he has lived all his life. I am extremely torn about letting go of this dream as I don't believe I could ever find a more idyllic location. However I could accept it a little easier if the property stays in the family and we are able to visit from time to time. It makes financial sense to sell at this time if the offer meets the valuation of the partners. I feel responsible for involving so many people in this venture and would hate to see anyone out of pocket as a result. Andre has suggested that he would only be interested in buying the entire property, selling his farm and home near Okanhandja and moving permanently to Ghaub rather than increase his share. We plan to meet with all parties once Andre agrees to meet the valuation which in essence gives everyone a modest return on their initial investment. Personally the decision is easy once Marian continues to have trouble with her eyes. The laser treatment which she underwent two years ago has never been a success despite her improved sight. Marian never complains and is extremely tolerant of discomfort so when she struggles with dry eye and strong direct sunlight is difficult for her the decision is easy. We will never realistically be in a position to relocate to Namibia. The climate would never work and the lack of suitable medical care close by makes it a non starter. It doesn't take long to decide and I agree with the other partners to accept Andre's offer.

Where to now? I was asked recently what the next project might be. Perhaps I will put it down as an incredible two year experience in an incredible country with great people who have helped me to fulfil a dream and realise an ambition and opportunity which might have been easier to pass on. Personally I believe I have found myself and the longing I carried has been satisfied. I feel energised by the experience and privileged to have lived in Africa for the best part of fifteen months. I would not change very much if I was starting again and it looks like from a business point of view the venture has been a success. The lodge is thriving with occupancy up nearly 100% which I am particularly pleased about. The long hours were worth it and Ghaub Guest Farm is now recognised among the leading affordable family lodges in Northern Namibia. The farm under Billy's and Andre's guidance has also enjoyed a profitable year with an excellent return from this years harvest while the cattle herd has been increased beyond expectation. I am thrilled that Ghaub looks like it will remain in the family for generations.

Just maybe I will now consider a new adventure and begin to think about the next challenge. My love of music has reached another level and I get terrific enjoyment out of listening to talented gifted musicians and songs that are well put together. I honestly regret not having seriously taken up an instrument years ago and persevering with it. I did take piano lessons at one stage but never with any great enthusiasm. I took up the guitar in my 20's but never really got past the basics although I still pick it up from time to time for my own amusement only. I always enjoyed a good drum and base beat and feel drawn even at this late stage to play around with it. My taste in music depends very much on the mood I am in. I can go from classical to hard rock to blues and then country in the space of a four hour car journey. When I was travelling I listened to music all the time and as mentioned have discovered a few artists and bands that I missed first time round. The Band has made a huge impression on me and The Last Waltz concert remains a favourite. I am particularly taken by the base player Rick Danko and the story of his life. I also recently discovered American country singer Iris DeMent who has the most incredible voice. Her duets with another favourite of mine John Prine are golden. Perhaps some day I will visit Nashville and fulfil another unrealised dream. Anything seems possible now. My head is full of ideas and I have enough material for several books or perhaps a play. It's as if my head is now clear and I can access my creative side as a result of this incredible experience.

This part of the story is drawing to a conclusion but I am struggling to let go of the dream. My priority is however to make sure that there are no regrets from any of those involved in this journey. My own family have been incredibly supportive and I would be delighted if the business proves to be a success. However I know I will never find another opportunity like this and it will be extremely difficult to step away from here. I have to believe that it will work out for the best and overall feel privileged to have had this opportunity. And by the way the best time to plant a tree was twenty years ago!